LETTERS

FROM THE SANDWICH ISLANDS

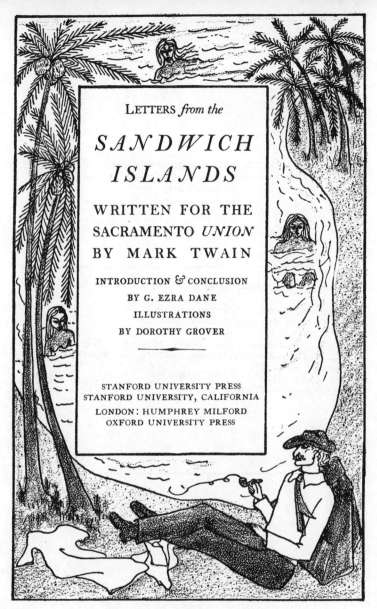

LETTERS *from the*

SANDWICH ISLANDS

WRITTEN FOR THE SACRAMENTO *UNION* BY MARK TWAIN

INTRODUCTION & CONCLUSION BY G. EZRA DANE

ILLUSTRATIONS BY DOROTHY GROVER

STANFORD UNIVERSITY PRESS
STANFORD UNIVERSITY, CALIFORNIA
LONDON: HUMPHREY MILFORD
OXFORD UNIVERSITY PRESS

HASKELL HOUSE PUBLISHERS LTD.
Publishers of Scarce Scholarly Books
NEW YORK. N. Y. 10012
1972

HASKELL HOUSE PUBLISHERS Ltd.
Publishers of Scarce Scholarly Books
280 LAFAYETTE STREET
NEW YORK, N. Y. 10012

Library of Congress Cataloging in Publication Data

Clemens, Samuel Langhorne, 1835-1910.
Letters from the Sandwich Islands.

1. Hawaii--Description and travel--To 1950.
2. Hawaii--Social life and customs. I. Sacramento
Union. II. Title.
DU623.C6 1972 919.69 72-2113
ISBN 0-8383-1471-6

Printed in the United States of America

CONTENTS

NOTE

This grateful acknowledgement is due to Miss Mabel R. Gillis, Librarian of the California State Library and to Miss Caroline Wenzel of its California Section for many indispensable references and helpful suggestions; to the Library of Hawaii and Miss Caroline P. Green for generously combing the files that yielded the long-lost letter to the *Daily Hawaiian Herald*, the priceless entry in the Volcano House Visitors' Book and the controversy with the rash editor of the *Commercial Advertiser*; to Mr. Edmond G. Kinyon, editor of the Grass Valley *Morning Union* for patient and fruitful search of the almost inaccessible files of the *Nevada Transcript*; to Mr. Lou Eichler of the Marysville *Appeal-Democrat* for similar assistance; and finally to the partner of my joys and sorrows for patience, unsparing criticism and faithful service at the typewriter.

G. E. D.

INTRODUCTION TO MARK TWAIN'S LETTERS FROM THE SANDWICH ISLANDS

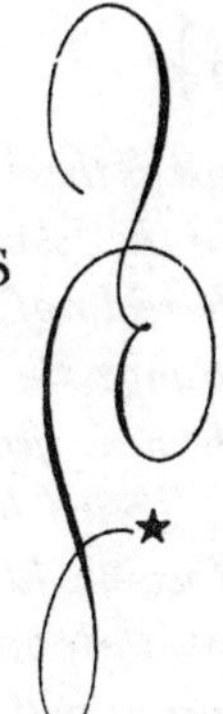

BY G. EZRA DANE

"I was young in those days, exceedingly young, marvelously young, younger than I am now, younger than I shall ever be again, by hundreds of years."

Autobiography, I, 245.

HE WAS THIRTY. *He had lived* Tom Sawyer *and* Huckleberry Finn *and* The Gilded Age *and* Life on the Mississippi *and most of* Roughing It. *But he had not written those books yet.*

He had not written any books, nor had he ever lectured. The trip to the Sandwich Islands that he made as correspondent of the Sacramento Union *in that spring and summer of* 1866 *was to furnish the subject of his first and most popular lecture. And if his original intention had been carried out, this book of letters from the Sandwich Islands would have been the first to bear the magic name, "Mark Twain."*

This is his first writing of travel; it is his first sustained writing of any kind. Most of it has never before been between covers. A portion was used to pad Roughing It *out to the great bulk required of a "subscription book" in the seventies; but it does not seem to belong with that lusty account of life in the mines and boom towns of the West. It is much more closely related to* The Innocents Abroad. *It immediately preceded and led, in the most direct manner, to that great book, which in its original form ran in a California newspaper just as these letters did. They tell of the Innocent's first trip abroad; for the Islands that are now a part of the United States were then the realm of His Majesty Kamehameha* V*—a land abounding in the strange, the beautiful and the absurd fully as much as any visited the next year by the steamer* Quaker City.

To tell how these letters came to be written is to tell of Mark Twain's literary beginnings. To explain why they have not come into their own as a book before is to tell of the sudden crowding of success and new opportunities that followed and submerged them.

The year 1866 *found Sam Clemens in San Francisco.*

He had been living by his pen for three and a half years—since the summer of 1862, *when the wild burlesques that he concocted for his own amusement and that of his fellow Nevada miners obtained him a regular berth on the audacious* Territorial Enterprise *of Virginia City. The complete unrestraint of that remarkable frontier paper had stimulated him to such monstrous journalistic hoaxes as the* Petrified Man *and the* Dutch Nick Massacre. *It had encouraged his natural talent for ridicule and improved the aim of his invective until resultant challenges and counter-challenges had got him and Steve Gillis afoul of the anti-dueling statutes. Then suddenly they had found it wise to put a mountain range between themselves and Nevada's new prison.*

Sam had been glad enough to get a reporter's job on the San Francisco Call, *but one of his spirit, who had known the freedom of the* Enterprise, *could not stand the irksome restrictions of political policy that controlled this paper. The work "was fearful drudgery—soulless drudgery—and almost destitute of interest. . . .an awful slavery for a lazy man." After a few months the employment had been terminated with no less willingness on his employer's part than on his.*

There was more satisfaction in contributing humorous sketches to Joe Laurence's pioneer weekly magazine, The Golden Era, *and then to the more sophisticated* Californian, *conducted by C. H. Webb and Bret Harte. Although they did not take themselves so seriously as the dignified eastern magazines, still these San Francisco periodicals had their ideals. Among those who wrote for them were some that essayed poetry and other forms of expression unquestionably literary. But the trend was toward something else, a distinctive thing that Bret Harte had and Prentice Mulford caught and that was the very character of Mark Twain. It had flashed out in the Gold Rush with John Phoenix and Old Block. Artemus Ward had the spirit of it on the platform, but he and Petroleum Vesuvius Nasby and the rest of the wartime humorists seemed to think that nothing would be recognized as funny in print unless cast in a jargon of misspelled and otherwise mangled English. What the San Franciscans discovered was that their western humor need not be illiterate. They were founding a new literature; but they did not know it, then.*

There was a lot of fun in writing for these little magazines but not enough pay to keep a man alive. It took a newspaper to do that. So when Sam Clemens and the Call *became mutually unbearable, Joe Goodman came to the rescue with a job and the opportunity Sam so sorely needed to vent his accumulated spleen in the columns of the* Enterprise, *as San Francisco correspondent. The phillipics that followed, against the San Francisco politicians and police, had made them itch for reprisal. Their opportunity came when little Fighting Steve Gillis was picked up for assault and Sam unsuspectingly went his bail and shipped him off to Virginia City. An attachment was issued against the obliging bondsman and Sam was in trouble with the law again.*

This time he had skipped to the Sierra. Steve Gillis' brother Jim had a cabin on Jackass Hill, in Tuolumne County, that was an ideal hideout. Sam had tried prospecting, but it was rainy on the Mother Lode that winter of '64 and '5 and much more suitable to sitting by the open fire in the cabin on the hill or around the stove at the hotel in Angel's Camp and swapping yarns. For here, during the quiet years that succeeded the Gold Rush, a folk lore developed that was American humor in its purest form. Jim Gillis was a consummate artist, who specialized in the tall story. He could lie his simple partner, Dick Stoker, and Stoker's cat, Tom Quartz, up to proportions fit for the fables he wove about them. Then there was old Ross Coon of Angel's who had told one afternoon, in the bar room, of Coleman and his wonderful jumping frog.

When, after the trouble was over and Sam was back at San Francisco, Artemus Ward asked him to contribute something for Ward's new book; this "villainous backwoods sketch," told in Ross Coon's dialect, had seemed appropriate to go with Ward's colloquial style. By fortunate mischance it had reached the publishers too late for burial in the Ward book, and without so much as by your leave had been published without copyright in the New York Saturday Press. *Copied by the newspapers far and wide, it swept across the country and back to California on a storm of shaking diaphragms.*

Mark Twain had scored a hit. It would take more than this to impress that pen-name on the mind of the nation. But one success in "the States" could give prestige in California. Mark Twain was by way of becoming a local celebrity at any rate. He received new consideration.

When the Pacific Mail Steamship Company inaugurated the first regular steamship service between San Francisco and Honolulu with its new steamer Ajax, *Mark Twain was offered a complimentary ticket. He declined because he felt bound to continue his correspondence for the* Enterprise. *But when the ship had gone he was so regretful and so fascinated with the idea of a trip to the romantic islands that he cast about for a way to earn his passage.*

The means for the journey were provided by the proprietors of the Sacramento Union, *then the greatest and most powerful journal in the West. The men who built it were James Anthony, the printer, Henry W. Larkin, and Paul Morrill, the brave and generous soul of the paper. It was Morrill who voiced the policy that made the* Union *so immensely popular with the people and so cordially hated by the political rings and public plunderers of the time. It was a policy that Sam Clemens could subscribe to:*

"Be just to everybody. Never strain the truth. Do not mince your words when you have to attack a great wrong. But above all things, the Union *is the friend of the common people! and the enemy of their enemies, high or low, rich or poor."*

Ella Sterling Cummins says of Morrill in her Story of the Files (*pp.* 78, 82-83):

"Personally he was a man of infinite depth of human sympathy, the best friend, husband, father; liberal to the poor [of which class Mark Twain was in 1866*]—giving without ostentation—And, if an enemy at all, one who never carried his enmity to an extreme, but who was always ready to forget and forgive an offense atoned for. In the very highest sense he was a gentleman. Open-handed as he was, he died not rich, though a man of less sterling principles occupying his position might have died a millionaire had he chosen."*

Such was the man who gave Mark Twain his start as a traveling correspondent, on his way toward The Innocents Abroad. *And Mark Twain never forgot the kindness. Many years later he said of Morrill and his partners that they were "lovable and well-beloved men; long ago dead, no doubt, but in me there is still one person who still holds them in grateful remembrance; for I dearly wanted to see the islands, and they gave me the opportunity when there was but slender likelihood that it could profit them in any way."*

Specifically, the agreement was, that they should pay him twenty dollars apiece for twenty or thirty weekly letters. They "hadn't any use for them," he said afterward, "but could afford to spend twenty dollars a week for nothing." (My Debut as a Literary Person,

Century Magazine, vol. 37, *pp.* 76-88, *Nov.*, 1899*; reprinted in collected works.)*

So it was that when the Ajax *set out from San Francisco on her second voyage, on March* 7, 1866, *her passenger list included the name "Mark Twain." The character that Sam Clemens had created for himself in print was beginning to absorb his identity.*

The story of the voyage is told in the first two letters. It was all rewritten for Roughing It, *where the three captains are merged in the Admiral, the disreputable Brown becomes Williams and, most curious of all, the stormy, seasick passage becomes serene and fine.*

It is very interesting, by the way, to compare various passages of the original Letters *as they appear here, with parallel passages from* Roughing It, *and to observe what changes were made six years later to suit the maturing style and more refined taste of the man who then knew he was writing for the whole English speaking world—and who was already being edited by "Livy," his wife. Perhaps the most remarkable fact that becomes evident on a detailed comparison is how much of the text remains unchanged. Most of what is best in the Sandwich Island chapters of* Roughing It *was taken practically verbatim from the* Letters. *The accounts of the various "equestrian excursions" aboard the remarkable steed "Oahu," the illustrated dissertations on the character and customs of the natives and some of the great descriptive passages are adopted with very little change. The difference consists principally in omission of old material, next, in addition of new, and least of all in alteration of what is carried over.*

The Letters *contain a total of about* 90,000 *words. The Sandwich Island material in* Roughing It *amounts to about* 35,000, *and more than* 5,000 *words of this is entirely new. Thus about two-thirds of the material contained in the* Letters *has lain unused in the* Union *files these seventy years. There are several reasons for this. If Mark Twain had carried out his original idea of publish-*

ing a book devoted entirely to the Sandwich Islands, he doubtless would have used nearly all of this material, either as it stood or more or less rewritten. But having put that idea aside and later finding himself faced with the necessity of filling a certain amount of space in Roughing It, *he took what was suitable and sufficient for that purpose and let the rest go. That foreclosed the possibility of a complete book on the subject and relegated the remaining material to the limbo of the files.*

Yet a great deal of that discarded material is fully as interesting and spirited as what was used. Indeed, some of it probably was left out of Roughing It *for the very reason that it was too spirited—in particular, the devastating ridicule directed at Minister Harris and other petty politicians. Other portions, of the best quality, such as the account of the second "equestrian excursion" from Honolulu and the description of the funeral ceremonies for the Princess Victoria, could only have been omitted for lack of room.*

He wrote twenty-five letters in all. Twenty-one of them are letters of travel, description, anecdote and human interest. These are all reproduced in this volume, rearranged in the sequence of Mark Twain's itinerary rather than the order of their publication. Three letters were written in discharge of the correspondent's specific mission to cover the Hawaiian trade. He did that job thoroughly, seriously and statistically in one letter on the Island trade generally, one on whaling and one on the sugar trade. They are good reports, but—or perhaps we should say because *they are good commercial reports—they have no literary quality. Hence (except for a portion of one) it has not seemed worthwhile to reproduce them here. They have little interest for any but scholars, and scholars, of course, would prefer to dig them from the files.* The remaining letter is Mark Twain's*

*Sacramento ***Weekly Union,*** vol. xv, no. 12, Apr. 21, 1866, p. 3, cols. 3-4, printed in part herein, p. 14; ib., no. 17, May 26, 1866, p. 6, cols. 4-6; ib., no. 35, Sept. 29, 1866, p. 3, cols. 2-5.

special report on the burning of the clipper ship Hornet *and the rescue of her starving survivors. Although this was a sensational scoop for the* Union, *obtained with the assistance of Minister Anson Burlingame and written under great pressure to catch the next day's mail to San Francisco, it is an item apart from the text of travel and description of the Islands, and has been omitted from this volume for the sake of continuity.**

But I must detain you no longer. It is sailing time on March 7, 1866. *The warning whistle has blown. The palatial steamer* Ajax *is about to leave her San Francisco wharf. All ashore what's going ashore! All aboard what's bound for the Sandwich Islands on the jolliest excursion ever made there!*

*It appeared in the Sacramento *Weekly Union*, vol. xv, no. 25, July 21, 1866, p. 1, cols. 4-7. Mark Twain used the same material several times afterward. An article written on the voyage homeward, *Forty-three days in an Open Boat,* was sent to Harpers as the budding author's first bid for literary distinction as represented by a genteel eastern magazine, where it appeared, to his chagrin, as the work of one Mark *Swain* (*Harpers*, vol. 34, pp. 104-113, Dec., 1866). See *My Debut as a Literary Person,* in the collected works, and *Autobiography*, vol. ii. pp. 121-125.

LETTERS

FROM THE SANDWICH ISLANDS

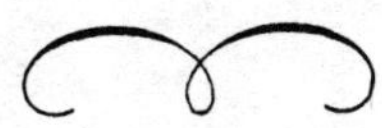

ON BOARD STEAMER AJAX

March 18, 1866

WE arrived here to-day at noon, and while I spent an hour or so talking, the other passengers exhausted all the lodging accommodations of Honolulu. So I must remain on board the ship to-night. It is very warm in the stateroom, no air enters the ports. Therefore, have dressed in a way which seems best calculated to suit the exigencies of the case. A description of this dress is not necessary. I may observe, however, that I bought the chief article of it at 'Ward's.'

There are a good many mosquitoes around to-night and they are rather troublesome; but it is a source of unalloyed satisfaction to me to know that the two millions I sat down on a minute ago will never sing again.

I will 'bunch' the first four or five days of my 'log' of this voyage and make up a few paragraphs therefrom.

We backed out from San Francisco at 4 P. M., all full—some full of tender regrets for severed associations, others full of buoyant anticipations of a pleasant voyage and a revivifying change of scene, and yet others full of schemes for extending their business relations and making larger profits. The balance were full of whisky. All except Brown. Brown had had a couple of peanuts for lunch, and therefore one could not say he was full of whisky, solely, without shamefully transcending the limits of truth.

Our little band of passengers were as well and thoughtfully cared for by the friends they left weeping upon the wharf as ever were any similar party of pilgrims. The traveling outfit conferred upon me began with a naval uniform, continued with a case of wine, a small assortment of medicinal liquors and brandy, several boxes of cigars, a bunch of matches, a fine-tooth comb and a cake of soap, and ended with a pair of socks. (N. B.—I gave the soap to Brown, who bit into it, and then shook his head and said that, 'as a general thing, he liked to prospect curious foreign dishes and find out what they were like, but he couldn't go that'—and threw it overboard.) This outfit is a fair sample of what our friends did for all of us. Three of our passengers—old sea-captains, whalers—Captain Cuttle, Captain Phelps and Captain Fitch (fictitious names)—had bought eight gallons of whisky, and their friends sent them eleven gallons more. (N. B.—Owing to head winds and a rough sea, this outfit did not hold out; the nineteen gallons were ample for the proposed eight-day voyage, but we were out upwards of ten days, you see. The whalers were all dry and unhappy this morning.)

Leaving all care and trouble and business behind in the city, now swinging gently around the hills and passing house by house and street by street out of view, we swept down through the Golden Gate and stretched away toward the shoreless horizon. It was a pleasant, breezy afternoon, and the strange new sense of entire and perfect emancipation from labor and responsibility coming strong upon me, I went up on the hurricane deck so that I could have room to enjoy it. I sat down on a bench, and for an hour I took a tranquil delight in that kind of labor which is such a luxury to the enlightened Christian—to wit the labor of other people. Captain Godfrey was 'making sail,' and he was moving the men around briskly. He made short work of the job, and his orders were marked by a felicity of language which challenged my admiration. Said he:

'Let go the main-hatch. Belay! Haul away on your tops'l jib! Belay! Clew up your top-gallants'l spanker-boom halliards! Belay! Port your gaff-tops'l sky-scrapers! Belay! Lively, you lubbers! Take a reef in the lee scuppers! Belay! Mr. Baxter, it's coming on to blow at about four bells in the hog-watch; have everything taut and trim for it. Belay!'

The ship was rolling fearfully. At this point I got up and started over to ask the Captain if it wouldn't be a good idea to belay a little for a change, but I fell down. I then resumed my former seat. For twenty minutes after this I took careful note of how the Captain leaned his body hard to port when the ship lurched to starboard, and hard to larboard when she lurched to port, and then got up to practice a little. I only met with moderate success, though, and after a few extraordinary evolutions, fetched up against the mainmast. The concussion did not injure the mast perceptibly, but if it had been a brick house the case might have been very different. I proceeded below, rather discouraged.

I found twenty-two passengers leaning over the bulwarks vomiting and remarking, 'Oh, my God!' and then vomiting again. Brown was there, ever kind and thoughtful, passing from one to another and saying, 'That's all right—that's all right, you know—it'll clean you out like a jug, and then you won't feel so ornery and smell so ridiculous.'

The sea was very rough for several days and nights, and the

vessel rolled and pitched heavily. All but six or eight of us took their meals in bed constantly, and remained shut up in the state-rooms day and night. The saloons and decks looked deserted and lonesome. But gradually the sea-sick unfortunates convalesced until our dinner complement was augmented to fifteen or twenty. There were frames or 'racks' on the tables to keep the dishes in their places, but they did not always succeed in doing it. An occasional heavy lurch would hoist out a dozen and start them prospecting for the deck. Brown was bitterly opposed to the racks, and said he 'Wasn't raised to eat out of them brick moulds.' No rack would answer for soup. The soup plate had to be held in the hand and nicely tilted from side to side to accommodate the fluid to the pitching of the ship. The chairs were not fastened to the floor, and it was fun to see a procession of gentlemen go sliding backwards to the bulkhead, holding their soup plates on a level with their breasts, and giving their whole attention to preventing the contents from splashing out. They would come back with the flow-tide and sail away again on the ebb. It would not do to set a glass of water down. The attentive waiters kept bringing water to Brown, who was always talking, and would not see the glass set down in time to make his remark heard: 'Frank, don't bring me any water; have to drink it at a gulp to keep it from spilling, and I've had more'n enough already.' And yet about once every two minutes some passenger opposite would put up his hands and shrink behind them and exclaim, 'Your water, Mr. Brown! your water! Look out for your water!' and lo, the suffering Brown would find his glass once more replenished and canting dangerously to leeward. It would be instantly seized and emptied. At the end of a quarter of an hour Brown had accomplished nothing in the way of dinner, on account of these incessant watery interruptions. The boy Frank brought another glass of water, and said, 'Will you have some beefsteak, Mr. Brown?' 'Take that water and go to blazes with it! Beefsteak! *no!* I've drank eleven gallons of water in fifteen minutes, and there ain't room enough in me for a sirloin steak off'm a sand-fly!'

Heaving my 'log,' I find the following entries on my tablets:

Wednesday, 7th—Left San Francisco at 4 P. M.; rough night.

Thursday—Weather still rough. Passengers nearly all sick; only half a dozen at breakfast out of thirty.

Friday—Strong gale all night; heavy sea on this evening; black overhead.

Saturday—Weather same, or more so.

You can take that four-days dose of your infamous 'Pacific,' Mr. Balboa, and digest it; and you may consider it well for your reputation in California that we had pretty fair weather the balance of the voyage. If we hadn't, I would have given you a blast in this letter that would have made your old dry bones rattle in your coffin—you shameless old foreign humbug!

MARK TWAIN

Reprinted from the Sacramento Weekly Union
April 21, 1866.

THE OLD NOR'WEST SWELL

March 19, 1866

ON the Sunday following our departure we had a fine day, and no wind scarcely, yet the sea ran high and the ship rolled a good deal. Upon inquiry, I learned that this was caused by the 'old nor'west swell,' which resembles any Broadway 'swell' in that it puts on a good many airs and conducts itself pretentiously even when it is not able to 'raise the wind.' The old nor'west swell, produced by the prevailing wind from that quarter, is always present in these seas, ever drifting on its eternal journey across the waters of the Pacific, year after year, and century after century as well, no doubt, and piling its billows aloft careless whether it be storm or calm. The wind and the swell both die out just above the equator. Another wind and another swell come up around Cape Horn from the opposite direction, and these die out just below the equator—so that a windless, waveless belt is left at the center of the earth, which marks the equator as distinctly as does the little black line on the map. Ships drift idly on that glassy sea, under the flaming sun of the tropics, for weeks together, without a breath of wind to flutter the drooping sails or fan the sweltering and blasphemous sailors.

We hear all our lives about the 'gentle, stormless Pacific,' and about the 'smooth and delightful route to the Sandwich Islands,' and about the 'steady blowing trades' that never vary, never change, never 'chop round,' and all the days of our boyhood we read how that infatuated old ass, Balboa, looked out from the top of a high rock upon a broad sea as calm and peaceful as a sylvan lake, and went into an ecstasy of delight, like any other Greaser over any other trifle, and shouted in his foreign tongue and waved his country's banner, and named his great discovery 'Pacific'—thus uttering a lie which will go on deceiving generation after generation of students while the old ocean lasts. If I had been there, with my experience, I would have said to this man Balboa, 'Now, if you think you have made a sufficient display of yourself, cavorting around on this conspicuous rock, you had better fold up your old rag and get back into the woods again, because you have jumped to a conclusion, and christened this sleeping boy-baby by a girl's name, without stopping to inquire into the sex of it.'

From all I can discover, if this foreign person had named this ocean the 'Four Months Pacific,' he would have come nearer the mark. My information is to the effect that the Summer months give fine weather, smooth seas and steady winds, with a month and a few days' good weather at the fag end of Spring and the beginning of Autumn; and that for the other seven or eight months of the year one can calculate pretty regularly on head winds and side winds and stern winds, and winds on the quarter, and winds several points abaft the beam, and winds that blow straight up from the bottom, and still other winds that come so straight down from above that the fore-stuns'l-spanker-jib-boom makes a hole through them as clean as a telescope.

And the sea rolls and leaps and chops and surges 'thortships' and up and down and fore-and-aft by turns, when the gales are blowing; and when they die out the old nor'west swell comes in and takes a hand, and stands a watch, and keeps up the marine earthquake until the winds are rested and ready to make trouble again.

In a word, the Pacific is 'rough' for seven or eight months in the year—not stormy, understand me—not what one could justly call stormy, but contrary, baffling and very 'rough.' Therefore, if that Balboa-constrictor had constructed a name for it that had 'Wild,' or 'Untamed,' to it, there would have been a majority of two months in the year in favor and in support of it.

If the Pacific were always pacific and its 'trades' blew steadily the year round, there would never be any necessity for steamers between Honolulu and San Francisco; but as it is, a trade is building up between the two ports, a considerable share of which is going to consist of fast freight and passengers, and only steamers can extend and develop this and conduct it successfully. You see, we plowed through the tangled seas and against the head winds this trip in a fraction over ten days, arriving a day after one of the fast clippers which left San Francisco a matter of three weeks before. The passage back, at this rate, is about five to seven days longer for the clipper, but not more than a day and a half or two days longer for the *Ajax*. You can rest assured that in the tremendous trade that is to spring up between California and the Islands during the next few years, the fast freight and passengers must be carried by steamers for seven or eight months in the year.

I will remark here that my information about the character of this ocean route is obtained from old ship-captains, one of whom has commanded in the packet trade for many years, and who has sailed these seas, whaling and otherwise, for forty-six years.

But the main argument in favor of a line of fast steamers is this: They would soon populate these islands with Americans, and loosen that French and English grip which is gradually closing around them, and which will result in a contest before many years as to which of the two shall seize and hold them. I leave America out of this contest, for her influence and her share in it have fallen gradually away until she is out in the cold now, and does not even play third fiddle to this European element.

But if California can send capitalists down here in seven or eight days time and take them back in nine or ten, she can fill these islands full of Americans and regain her lost foothold. Hawaii is too far away now, though, when it takes a man twenty days to come here and twenty-five or thirty to get back again in a sailing vessel.

The steamer line ought to be established, even if it should lose money for two years. Your State has never paid one single dollar of profit to the United States—you are nothing but a burden and an expense to the country—but the kingdom of Hawaii, without costing the United States a cent, has paid her, in customs, $400,000 in a single year.

California's profits from this section can be made greater and far more lasting than those from Montana. Therefore let your Merchants' Exchange look after the former just as earnestly as they are doing with the latter.

In writing about sea voyages it is customary to state, with the blandest air of conveying information of rare freshness and originality, that anything, however trivial, that promises to spice the weary monotony of the voyage with a new sensation, is eagerly seized upon and the most made of it by the passengers. I decline to insult your intelligence by making this threadbare statement, preferring to believe you would easily divine the existence of the fact without having to be told it.

We had a bullock tied up on the forecastle, and a box near by with two sheep and a pig in it. These animals afforded a trifling amusement for us on our fair days, and when the opportunity offered we used to go forward and worry them. The bullock was always down on his beam-ends. If he ever dared to get up on his feet for a second in stormy weather, the next lurch of the ship would 'snatch him bald-headed,' as Mr. Brown expressed it, and flop him flat on the deck; and in fair weather he was seldom able to get up, on account of his sore bones, acquired through the bangs and bruises of his foul weather experiences. So the bullock lay down pretty much all the time from San Francisco to Honolulu—and ever as his wandering gaze rested upon reeling men, and plunging ship and towering billow, his eloquent eye damned the weather.

Said Mr. Brown, once: 'Let's go forward and twist the Captain's tail.'

'Who? Captain Godfrey?'

'Thunder! no; Captain Gordon.'

'Who?'

'Why, the bullock—Captain Gordon. We call him Captain Gordon because he lays down so much.'

I recognized the point of Mr. Brown's facetiousness then. Captain Gordon, a not undistinguished officer of the Eastern armies, had kept his room all the way, but as he was unwell enough to prefer that course to staggering about the tossing decks, and had a right to do as he pleased anyhow, I reprimanded Brown on the spot for his inconsiderate levity.

The pig was pulled and hauled and cuffed for the amusement of the idle passengers, but unknown to himself he had his revenge; for he imparted such a villainous odor of the sty to the hands and clothing of any man who meddled with him, that that man could never drift to windward of a lady passenger without suffering disgrace and humiliation under the rebuke of her offended upturned nose. The pig had no name. This was a source of ceaseless regret to Mr. Brown, and he often spoke of it. At last one of the sailors named it, and Brown happened to be passing by and overheard him. The sailor was feeding the animals, and the pig kept crowding the sheep away and monopolizing the slop pail. The sailor rapped him on the nose and said:

'Oh, go way wid you, Dinnis.'

To have heard the passengers go into explosions of laughter when Brown rushed in, in a state of wild excitement, and re-related this circumstance, one might have supposed that this ship had been sailing round and round the world for dreary ages, and that this was the first funny circumstance that had ever blessed with a gleam of cheerfulness the dismal voyage. But, as other writers have said before, even so diluted a thing as this can send a thrill of delight through minds and bodies growing torpid under the dull sameness of a long sea voyage.

From that day forward it was Dennis here, and Dennis there, and Dennis everywhere. Dennis was in everybody's mouth; Dennis was mentioned twice where the everlasting wonder, 'how many miles we made yesterday,' was expressed once. A stranger's curiosity would have been excited to the last degree to know who this rival to General Grant in notoriety was, that had so suddenly sprung up—this so thoroughly canvassed, discussed, and popular 'Dennis.' But on the 16th of March Dennis was secretly executed by order of the steward, and Brown said that when the fact became generally known, there was not a dry eye in the ship. He fully believed what he said, too. He has a generous heart and a fervent imagination, and a capacity for creating impossible facts and then implicitly believing them himself, which is perfectly marvelous.

Dennis was served up on the 17th for our St. Patrick's dinner, and gave me a stomach-ache that lasted twenty-four hours. In life he was lovely, and behold, he was powerful in death. Peace to his ashes!

The most steady-going amusement the gentlemen had on the trip was euchre, and the most steady-going the ladies had was being sea-sick. For days and nights together we used to sit in the smoking room and play euchre on the same table so sacredly devoted to 'seven-up' by the livelier set of passengers who traveled last voyage in the *Ajax*. It took me some little time to learn to play euchre with those old sea-captains, because they brought in so many terms that are neither in Hoyle nor the dictionary. Hear how they talked:

Captain Fitch—'Who hove that ace on there?'

Captain Phelps—'Why, I did.'

Captain Cuttle—'No, you didn't, either; I hove it myself.'

Captain Phelps—'You didn't, by the Eternal!—you hove the king.'

Captain Fitch—'Well, now, that's just the way—always jawin' about who hove this and who hove that—always sailin' on a taut bowlin'. Why can't you go slow? You keep heavin' on 'em down so fast that a man can't tell nothing about it.'

Captain Phelps—'Well, I don't care—let it go—I can stand it, I cal'late. Here goes for a euchre!' (Here the Captain played an odd-suit ace.) 'Swing your bower if you've got it, but I'll take them last three tricks or break a rope-yarn.'

(I, as partner to Captain Phelps, get bewildered and make a bad play.)

Captain Phelps—'Now what did you trump my ace for? that ain't any way to do; you're always a-sailin' too close to the wind.'

(In a moment or two I make another bad play.)

Captain Phelps—'Ger-reat Scotland! what in the nation you dumpin' that blubber at such a time as this for? Rip! I knowed it! took with a nine-spot! royals, stuns'ls—everything, gone to smash, and nobody euchred!'

It is necessary to explain that those ancient, incomprehensible whalers always called worthless odd-suit cards 'blubber.'

We passengers are all at home now—taking meals at the American Hotel, and sleeping in neat white cottages, buried in noble shade trees and enchanting tropical flowers and shrubs.

MARK TWAIN

Reprinted from the Sacramento Weekly Union
April 21, 1866.

THE STEAMSHIP AJAX

March — 1866.

I HAVE been here a day or two now, but I do not know enough concerning the country yet to commence writing about it with confidence, so I will drift back to sea again.

The *Ajax* is a 2,000 ton propeller, and one of the strongest built vessels afloat. All her timber-work is very heavy and fastened and bolted together as if to hold for a century. She was intended for a war-ship, and this accounts for her extraordinary strength. She has excellent cabin accommodations for sixty passengers, without crowding, and bunks for forty more. She has room for over twelve hundred tons of freight after her coal and stores for the round trip are all in; and when a coal depot is established for her hereafter at Honolulu, so that she need carry only fuel enough for half the voyage, she can take two or three hundred tons more. Her principal officers all served in the war. Captain Godfrey and the Chief Mate, Baxter, were both in our navy, and Sanford, the Chief Engineer, has seen a great deal of service. He held his commission as Chief Engineer in the navy for sixteen years, and was in seven battles in the Mexican war, and six during the rebellion—a very good record. Hite, the Purser, served under General Sherman, in the Paymaster's department, with the rank of Captain.

The *Ajax* has a 'harp' engine, laid horizontally, so as to be entirely below the water line—a judicious arrangement, in view of the ship's intended duty originally, in a service where cannon balls and shells would pelt her, instead of the rain showers of the Pacific. The horizontal engine takes up much less room than when placed in an upright position; it packs as closely as sardines in a box and gives the ship a good deal of extra space for freight and passengers. Every portion of the *Ajax's* engine and fire rooms is kept in perfect neatness and good order by the Chief's crew of eighteen men.

In this place I would drop a hint of caution to all romantic young people who yearn to become bold sailor boys and ship as firemen on a steamer. Such a berth has its little drawbacks—inconveniences which not all the romance in the world can reconcile one to. The principal of these is the sultry temperature of the furnace room, where the fireman, far below the surface of the sea and away from the fresh air and the light of day, stands in a narrow space between two rows of furnaces that flame and glare like the fires of hell, and shovels coal four hours at a stretch in an unvarying temperature of 148 degrees Fahrenheit! And yet how the people of Honolulu growl and sweat on an uncommonly warm day, with the mercury at 82 degrees in the shade and somewhere in the neighborhood of 100 degrees in the sun! Steamer firemen do not live, on an average, over 5 years.

MARK TWAIN

Reprinted from the Sacramento Weekly Union
April 21, 1866.

ARRIVAL AT HONOLULU

March—
1866.

WE came in sight of two of this group of islands, Oahu and Molokai (pronounced O-waw-hoo and Mollo-*ki*), on the morning of the 18th, and soon exchanged the dark blue waters of the deep sea for the brilliant light blue of 'soundings.' The fat, ugly birds (said to be a species of albatross) which had skimmed after us on tireless wings clear across the ocean, left us, and an occasional flying-fish went skimming over the water in their stead. Oahu loomed high, rugged, treeless, barren, black and dreary, out of the sea, and in the distance Molokai lay like a homely sway-back whale on the water.

As we rounded the promontory of Diamond Head (bringing into view a grove of cocoa-nut trees, first ocular proof that we were in the tropics), we ran up the stars and stripes at the main-spencer-gaff, and the Hawaiian flag at the fore. The latter is suggestive of the prominent political elements of the Islands. It is part French, part English, part American, and is Hawaiian in general. The union is the English cross; the remainder of the flag (horizontal stripes) looks American, but has a blue French stripe in addition to our red and white ones. The flag was gotten up by foreign legations in council with the Hawaiian Government. The eight stripes refer to the eight islands which are inhabited; the other four are barren rocks incapable of supporting a population.

As we came in sight we fired a gun, and a good part of Honolulu turned out to welcome the steamer. It was Sunday morning, and about church time, and we steamed through the narrow channel to the music of six different church bells, which sent their mellow tones far and wide, over hills and valleys, which were peopled by naked, savage, thundering barbarians only fifty years ago! Six Christian churches within five miles of the ruins of a Pagan temple, where human sacrifices were daily offered up to hideous idols in the last century! We were within pistol shot of one of a group of islands whose ferocious inhabitants closed in upon the doomed and helpless Captain Cook and murdered him, eighty-seven years ago; and lo! their descendants were at church! Behold what the missionaries have wrought!

By the time we had worked our slow way up to the wharf, under the guidance of McIntyre, the pilot, a mixed crowd of four or five hundred people had assembled—Chinamen, in the costume of their country; foreigners and the better class of natives, and 'half whites' in carriages and dressed in Sacramento Summer fashion; other native men on foot, some in the cast-off clothing of white folks, and a few wearing a battered hat, an old ragged vest, and nothing else—at least nothing but an unnecessarily slender rag passed between the legs; native women clad in a single garment—a bright colored robe or wrapper as voluminous as a balloon, with full sleeves. This robe is 'gathered' from shoulder to shoulder, before and behind, and then descends in ample folds to the feet—seldom a chemise or any other undergarment—fits like a circus tent fits the tent pole, and no hoops. These robes were bright yellow, or bright crimson, or pure black occasionally, or gleaming white; but 'solid colors' and 'stunning' ones were the rule. They wore little hats such as the sex wear in your cities, and some of the younger women had very pretty faces and splendid black eyes and heavy masses of long black hair, occasionally put up in a 'net;' some of these dark, gingerbread colored beauties were on foot—generally on barefoot, I may add—and others were on horseback—astraddle; they never ride any other way, and they ought to know which way is best, for there are no more accomplished horsewomen in the world, it is said. The balance of the crowd consisted chiefly of little half-naked native boys and girls. All were chattering in the catchy, chopped-up Kanaka language; but what they were chattering about will always remain a mystery to me.

Captain Fitch said, 'There's the King! that's him in the buggy; I know him far as I can see him.'

I had never seen a King in my life, and I naturally took out my note-book and put him down: 'Tall, slender, dark; full-bearded; green frock coat, with lappels and collar bordered with gold band an inch wide; plug hat—broad gold band around it; royal costume looks too much like a livery; this man isn't as fleshy as I thought he was.'

I had just got these notes entered when Captain Fitch discovered that he had got hold of the wrong King—or, rather, that he had got hold of the King's driver or a carriage-driver of one of the nobility. The King was not present at all. It was a great disappointment to me. I heard afterward that the comfortable, easy going King Kamehameha (pronounced Ka-may-ah-may-ah) V had been seen sitting on a barrel on the wharf, the day before, fishing; but there was no consolation in that; that did not restore to me my lost King.

The town of Honolulu (said to contain between 12,000 and 15,000 inhabitants) is spread over a dead level; has streets from twenty to thirty feet wide, solid and level as a floor, most of them straight as a line and a few as crooked as a corkscrew; houses one and two stories high, built of wood, straw, 'dobies and dull cream-colored pebble-and-shell-conglomerated coral cut into oblong square blocks and laid in cement, but no brick houses; there are great yards, more like plazas, about a large number of the dwelling-houses, and these are carpeted with bright green grass, into which your foot sinks out of sight; and they are ornamented by a hundred species of beautiful flowers and blossoming shrubs, and shaded by noble tamarind trees and the 'Pride of India,' with its fragrant flower, and by the 'Umbrella Tree,' and I do not know how many more. I had rather smell Honolulu at sunset than the old Police Courtroom in San Francisco.

I had not shaved since I left San Francisco—ten days. As soon as I got ashore I hunted for a striped pole, and shortly found one. I always had a yearning to be a King. This may never be, I suppose. But at any rate it will always be a satisfaction to me to know that if I am not a King, I am the next thing to it—I have been shaved by the King's barber.

Walking about on shore was very uncomfortable at first; there was no spring to the solid ground, and I missed the heaving and rolling of the ship's deck; it was unpleasant to lean unconsciously to an anticipated lurch of the world and find that the world did not lurch, as it should have done. And there was something else missed—something gone—something wanting, I could not tell what—a dismal vacuum of some kind or other—a sense of emptiness. But I found out what it was presently. It was the absence of the ceaseless dull hum of beating waves and whipping sails and fluttering of the propeller, and creaking of the ship—sounds I had become so accustomed to that I had ceased to notice them and had become unaware of their existance until the deep Sunday stillness on shore made me vaguely conscious that a familiar spirit of some kind or other was gone from me. Walking on the solid earth with legs used to the 'giving' of the decks under his tread, made Brown sick, and he went off to bed and left me to wander alone about this odd-looking city of the tropics.

The further I traveled through the town the better I liked it. Every step revealed a new contrast—disclosed something I was unaccustomed to. In place of the grand mud-colored brown stone fronts of San Francisco, I saw neat white cottages, with green window-shutters; in place of front yards like billiard-tables with iron fences around them, I saw those cottages surrounded by ample yards, about like Portsmouth Square (as to size), thickly clad with green grass, and shaded by tall trees, through whose dense foliage the sun could scarcely penetrate; in place of the customary infernal geranium languishing in dust and general debility on tin-roofed rear additions or in bedroom windows, I saw luxurious banks and thickets of flowers, fresh as a meadow after a rain, and glowing with the richest dyes; in place of the dingy horrors of the 'Willows,' and the painful sharp-pointed shrubbery of that funny caricature of nature which they call 'South Park,' I saw huge-bodied, wide-spreading forest trees, with strange names and stranger appearance—trees that cast a shadow like a thunder-cloud, and were able to stand alone without being tied to green poles; in place of those vile, tiresome, stupid, everlasting gold-fish, wiggling around in glass globes and assuming all shades and degrees of distortion through the magnifying and diminishing qualities of their transparent prison houses, I saw cats—Tom-cats, Mary-Ann cats, long-tailed cats, bob-tailed cats, blind cats, one-eyed cats, wall-eyed cats, cross-eyed cats, grey cats, black cats, white cats, yellow cats, striped cats, spotted cats, tame cats, wild cats, singed cats, individual cats, groups of cats, platoons of cats, companies of cats, regiments of cats, armies of cats, multitudes of cats, millions of cats, and all of them sleek, fat, lazy and sound asleep; in place of roughs and rowdies staring and blackguarding on the corners, I saw long-haired, saddle-colored Sandwich Island maidens sitting on the ground in the shade of corner houses, gazing indolently at whatever or whoever happened along; instead of that wretched cobble-stone pavement nuisance, I walked on a firm foundation of coral, built up from the bottom of the sea by the absurd but persevering insect of that name, with a light layer of lava and cinders overlying the coral, belched up out of fathomless hell long ago through the seared and blackened crater that stands dead and cold and harmless yonder in the distance now; instead of the cramped and crowded street-cars, I met dusky native women sweeping by, free as the wind, on fleet horses and astraddle, with gaudy riding-sashes streaming like banners behind them; instead of the combined stenches of Sacramento street, Chinadom and Brannan street slaughter-houses, I breathed the balmy fragrance of jessamine, oleander, and the Pride of India; in place of the hurry and bustle and noisy confusion of San Francisco, I moved in the midst of a Summer calm as tranquil as dawn in the Garden of Eden; in place of our familiar skirting sand hills and the placid bay, I saw on the one side a framework of tall, precipitous mountains close at hand, clad in refreshing green, and cleft by deep, cool, chasm-like valleys—and in front the grand sweep of the ocean; a brilliant, transparent green near the shore, bound and bordered by a long white line of foamy spray dashing against the reef, and further out the dead, blue water of the deep sea, flecked with 'white caps,' and in the far horizon a single, lonely sail—

At this moment, this man Brown, who has no better manners than to read over one's shoulder, observes:

'Yes, and hot. Oh, I reckon not (only 82 in the shade)! Go on, now, and put it all down, now that you've begun; just say, "And more 'santipedes,' and cockroaches, and fleas, and lizards, and red ants, and scorpions, and spiders, and mosquitoes and missionaries"—oh, blame my cats if I'd live here two months, not if I was High-You-Muck-a-Muck and King of Wawhoo, and had a harem full of hyenas!' (Wahine [most generally pronounced Wyheeny], seems to answer for wife, woman and female of questionable character, indifferently. I never can get this man Brown to understand that 'hyena' is not the proper pronunciation. He says 'It ain't any odds; it describes some of 'em, anyway.')

I remarked: 'But, Mr. Brown, these are trifles.'

'Trifles be—blowed! You get nipped by one of them scorpions once, and see how you like it! There was Mrs. Jones, swabbing her face with a sponge; she felt something grab her cheek; she dropped the sponge and out popped a scorpion an inch and a half long! Well, she just got up and danced the Highland fling for two hours and a half—and yell!—why, you could have heard her from Lu-wow to Hoola-hoola, with the wind fair! and for three days she soaked her cheek in brandy and salt, and it swelled up as big as your two fists. And you want to know what made me light out of bed so sudden last night? Only a "santipede"—nothing, only a "santipede," with forty-two legs on a side, and every foot hot enough to burn a hole through a raw-hide. Don't you know one of them things grabbed Miss Boone's foot when she was riding one day? He was hid in the stirrip, and just clamped himself around her foot and sunk his fangs plum through her shoe; and she just throwed her whole soul into one war-whoop and then fainted. And she didn't get out of bed nor set that foot on the floor again for three weeks. And how did Captain Godfrey always get off so easy? Why, because he always carried a bottle full of scorpions and santipedes soaked in alcohol, and whenever he got bit he bathed the place with that devilish mixture or took a drink out of it, I don't recollect which. And how did he have to do once, when he hadn't his bottle along? He had to cut out the bite with his knife and fill up the hole with arnica, and then prop his mouth open with the boot-jack to keep from getting the lockjaw. Oh, fill me up about this lovely country! You can go on writing that slop about balmy breezes and fragrant flowers, and all that sort of truck, but you're not going to leave out them santipedes and things for want of being reminded of it, you know.'

I said, mildly: 'But, Mr. Brown, these are the mere—'

'Mere—your grandmother! they ain't the mere anything! What's the use of you telling me they're the mere—mere—whatever it was you was going to call it? You look at them raw splotches all over my face—all over my arms—all over my body! Mosquito bites! Don't tell me about mere—mere things! You can't get around them mosquito bites. I took and brushed out my bar good night before last, and tucked it in all around, and before morning I was eternally chawed up, anyhow. And the night before I fastened her up all right, and got into bed and smoked that old strong pipe until I got strangled and smothered and couldn't get out, and then they swarmed in and jammed their bills through my shirt and sucked me as dry as a life-preserver before I got my breath again. And how did that deadfall work? I was two days making it, and sweated two buckets full of brine, and blame the mosquito ever went under it; and sloshing around in my sleep I ketched my foot in it and got it flattened out so that it wouldn't go into a green turtle shell forty-four inches across the back. Jim Ayres grinding out seven double verses of poetry about Wah-*hoo!* and crying about leaving the blasted place in the two last verses; and you slobbering here about—there you are! Now—*now*, what do you say? That yellow spider could straddle over a saucer just like nothing—and if I hadn't been here to set that spittoon on him, he would have been between your sheets in a minute—he was traveling straight for your bed—he had his eye on it. Just pull at that web that he's been stringing after him—pretty near as hard to break as sewing silk; and look at his feet sticking out all round the spittoon. Oh, confound Waw-*hoo!*"

I am glad Brown has got disgusted at that murdered spider and gone; I don't like to be interrupted when I am writing—especially by Brown, who is one of those men who always looks at the unpleasant side of everything, and I seldom do.

MARK TWAIN

Reprinted from the Sacramento Weekly Union
April 21, 1866.

LIVING CONDITIONS

March—
1866.

I DID NOT expect to find as comfortable a hotel as the American, with its large, airy, well-furnished rooms, distinguished by perfect neatness and cleanliness, its cool, commodious verandas, its excellent table, its ample front yard, carpeted with grass and adorned with shrubbery, *et cetera*—and so I was agreeably disappointed. One of our lady passengers from San Francisco, who brings high recommendations, has purchased a half interest in the hotel, and she shows such a determination to earn success that I heartily wish she may achieve it—and the more so because she is an American, and if common remark can be depended upon the foreign element here will not allow an American to succeed if a good strong struggle can prevent it.

Several of us have taken rooms in a cottage in the center of the town, and are well satisfied with our quarters. There is a grassy yard as large as Platt's Hall on each of three sides of the premises; a number of great tamarind and algeraba trees tower above us, and their dense, wide-spreading foliage casts a shade that palls our verandas with a sort of solemn twilight, even at noonday. If I were not so fond of looking into the rich masses of green leaves that swathe the stately tamarind right before my door, I would idle less and write more, I think. The leaf of this tree is of the size and shape of that of our sickly, homely locust in the States; but the tamarind is as much more superb a tree than the locust as a beautiful white woman is more lovely than a Digger squaw who may chance to generally resemble her in shape and size.

The algeraba (my spelling is guess-work) has a gnarled and twisted trunk, as thick as a barrel, far-reaching, crooked branches and a delicate, feathery foliage which would be much better suited to a garden shrub than to so large a tree.

We have got some handsome mango trees about us also, with dark green leaves, as long as a goose quill and not more than twice as broad. The trunk of the tree is about six inches through, and is very straight and smooth. Five feet from the ground it divides into three branches of equal size, which bend out with a graceful curve and then assume an upright position. From these numerous smaller branches sprout. The main branches are not always three in number, I believe; but ours have this characteristic, at any rate.

We pay from five to seven dollars a week for furnished rooms, and ten dollars for board.

Mr. Laller, an American, and well spoken of, keeps a restaurant where meals can be had at all hours. So you see that folks of both regular and eccentric habits can be accommodated in Honolulu.

Washing is done chiefly by the natives; price, a dollar a dozen. If you are not watchful, though, your shirt won't stand more than one washing, because Kanaka artists work by a most destructive method. They use only cold water—sit down by a brook, soap the garment, lay it on one rock and 'pound' it with another. This gives a shirt a handsome fringe around its borders, but it is ruinous on buttons. If your washerwoman knows you will not put up with this sort of thing, however, she will do her pounding with a bottle, or else rub your clothes clean with her hands. After the garments are washed the artist spreads them on the green grass, and the flaming sun and the winds soon bleach them as white as snow. They are then ironed on a cocoa-leaf mat spread on the ground, and the job is finished. I cannot discover that anything of the nature of starch is used.

Board, lodging, clean clothes, furnished room, coal oil or whale oil lamp (dingy, greasy, villainous)—next you want water, fruit, tobacco and cigars, and possibly wines and liquors—and then you are 'fixed,' and ready to live in Honolulu.

The water is pure, sweet, cool, clear as crystal, and comes from a spring in the mountains, and is distributed all over the town through leaden pipes. You can find a hydrant spirting away at the bases of three or four trees in a single yard, sometimes, so plenty and cheap is this excellent water. Only twenty-four dollars a year supplies a whole household with a limitless quantity of it.

You must have fruit. You feel the want of it here. At any rate, I do, though I cared nothing whatever for it in San Francisco. You pay about twenty-five cents ('two reals,' in the language of the country, borrowed from Mexico, where a good deal of their silver money comes from) a dozen for oranges; and so delicious are they that some people frequently eat a good many at luncheon. I seldom eat more than ten or fifteen at a sitting, however, because I despise to see anybody gormandize. Even fifteen is a little surprising to me, though, for two or three oranges in succession were about as much as I could ever relish at home. Bananas are worth about a bit a dozen—enough for that rather over-rated fruit. Strawberries are plenty, and as cheap as the bananas. Those which are carefully cultivated here have a far finer flavor than the California article. They are in season a good part of the year. I have a kind of a general idea that the tamarinds are rather sour this year. I had a curiosity to taste these things, and I knocked half a dozen off the tree and eat them the other day. They sharpened my teeth up like a razor, and put a 'wire edge' on them that I think likely will wear off when the enamel does. My judgment now is that when it comes to sublimated sourness, persimmons will have to take a back seat and let the tamarinds come to the front. They are shaped and colored like a pea-nut, and about three times as large. The seeds inside of the thin pod are covered with that sour, gluey substance which I experimented on. They say tamarinds make excellent preserves (and by a wise provision of Providence, they are generally placed in sugar-growing countries), and also that a few of them placed in impure water at sea will render it palatable. Mangoes and guavas are plenty. I do not like them. The limes are excellent, but not very plenty. Most of the apples that are brought to this market are imported from Oregon. Those I have eaten were as good as bad turnips, but not better. They claim to raise good apples and peaches on some of these islands. I have not seen any grapes or pears or melons here. They may be out of season, but I keep thinking it is dead Summer time now.

The only cigars smoked here are those trifling, insipid, tasteless, flavorless things they call 'Manilas'—ten for twenty-five cents; and it would take a thousand to be worth half the money. After you have smoked about thirty-five dollars' worth of them in a forenoon you feel nothing but a desperate yearning to go out somewhere and take a smoke. They say high duties and a sparse population render it unprofitable to import good cigars, but I do not see why some enterprising citizen does not manufacture them from the native tobacco. A Kanaka gave me some Oahu tobacco yesterday, of fine texture, pretty good flavor, and so strong that one pipe full of it satisfied me for several hours. (This man Brown has just come in and says he has bought a couple of tons of Manilas to smoke to-night.)

Wines and liquors can be had in abundance, but not of the very best quality. The duty on brandy and whisky amounts to about three dollars a gallon, and on wines from thirty to sixty cents a bottle, according to market value. And just here I would caution Californians who design visiting these islands against bringing wines or liquors with their baggage, lest they provoke the confiscation of the latter. They will be told that to uncork the bottles and take a little of the contents out will compass the disabilities of the law, but they may find it dangerous to act upon such a suggestion, which is nothing but an unworthy evasion of the law, at best. It is incumbent upon the custom officers to open trunks and search for contraband articles, and although I think the spirit of the law means to permit foreigners to bring a little wine or liquor ashore for private use, I know the letter of it allows nothing of the kind. In addition to searching a passenger's baggage, the custom-house officer makes him swear that he has got nothing contraband with him. I will also mention, as a matter of information, that a small sum (two dollars for each person) is exacted for permission to land baggage, and this goes to the support of the hospitals.

I have said that the wines and liquors sold here are not of the best quality. It could not well be otherwise, as I can show. There seem to be no hard, regular drinkers in this town, or at least very few; you perceive that the duties are high; saloon keepers pay a license of a thousand dollars a year; they must close up at ten o'clock at night and not open again before daylight the next morning; they are not allowed to open on Sunday at all. These laws are very strict, and are rigidly obeyed.

I must come back to water again, though I thought I had exhausted the subject. As no ice is kept here, and as the notion that snow is brought to Honolulu from the prodigious mountains on the island of Hawaii is a happy fiction of some imaginative writer, the water used for drinking is usually kept cool by putting it in 'monkeys' and placing those animals in open windows, where the breezes of heaven may blow upon them. 'Monkeys' are slender-necked, large-bodied, gourd-shaped earthenware vessels, manufactured in Germany, and are popularly supposed to keep water very cool and fresh, but I cannot indorse that supposition. If a wet blanket were wrapped around the monkey, I think the evaporation would cool the water within, but nobody seems to consider it worth while to go to that trouble, and I include myself among this number.

Ice is worth a hundred dollars a ton in San Francisco, and five or six hundred here, and if the steamer continues to run, a profitable trade may possibly be driven in the article hereafter. It does not pay to bring it from Sitka in sailing vessels, though. It has been tried. It proved a mutinous and demoralizing cargo, too; for the sailors drank the melted freight and got so high-toned that they refused ever afterwards to go to sea unless the captains would guarantee them ice-water on the voyage. Brown got the latter fact from Captain Phelps, and says he 'coppered it in consideration of the source.' To 'copper' a thing, he informs me, is to bet against it.

If you get into conversation with a stranger in Honolulu, and experience that natural desire to know what sort of ground you are treading on by finding out what manner of man your stranger is, strike out boldly and address him as 'Captain.' Watch him narrowly, and if you see by his countenance that you are on the wrong tack, ask him where he preaches. It is a safe bet that he is either a missionary or captain of a whaler. I am now personally acquainted with seventy-two captains and ninety-six missionaries. The captains and ministers form one-half of the population; the third fourth is composed of common Kanakas and mercantile foreigners and their families, and the final fourth is made up of high officers of the Hawaiian Government. And there are just about cats enough for three apiece all around.

A solemn stranger met me in the suburbs yesterday and said: 'Good morning, your reverence. Preach in the stone church yonder, no doubt?'

'No, I don't. I'm not a preacher.'

'Really, I beg your pardon, Captain. I trust you had a good season. How much oil—'

'Oil? Why, what do you take me for? I'm not a whaler.'

'Oh, I beg a thousand pardons, your Excellency. Major-General in the household troops, no doubt? Minister of the Interior, likely? Secretary of War? First Gentleman of the Bedchamber? Commissioner of the Royal—'

'Stuff! man. I'm no official. I'm not connected in any way with the Government.'

'Bless my life! Then, who the mischief are you? what the mischief are you? and how the mischief did you get here, and where in thunder did you come from?'

'I'm only a private personage—an unassuming stranger—lately arrived from America.'

'No! Not a missionary! not a whaler! not a member of His Majesty's Government! not even Secretary of the Navy! Ah, Heaven! it is too blissful to be true; alas, I do but dream. And yet that noble, honest countenance—those oblique, ingenuous eyes—that massive head, incapable of—of—anything; your hand; give me your hand, bright waif. Excuse these tears. For sixteen weary years I have yearned for a moment like this, and—'

Here his feelings were too much for him, and he swooned away. I pitied this poor creature from the bottom of my heart. I was deeply moved. I shed a few tears on him and kissed him for his mother. I then took what small change he had on him and 'shoved.'

Mark Twain

Reprinted from the Sacramento Weekly Union
April 21, 1866.

EQUESTRIAN EXCURSION

March—
1866.

I AM probably the most sensitive man in the kingdom of Hawaii to-night—especially about sitting down in the presence of my betters. I have ridden fifteen or twenty miles on horseback since 5 P.M., and to tell the honest truth, I have a delicacy about sitting down at all. I am one of the poorest horsemen in the world, and I never mount a horse without experiencing a sort of dread that I may be setting out on that last mysterious journey which all of us must take sooner or later, and I never come back in safety from a horseback trip without thinking of my latter end for two or three days afterward. This same old regular devotional sentiment began just as soon as I sat down here five minutes ago.

An excursion to Diamond Head and the King's Cocoanut Grove was planned to-day—time, 4:30 P.M.—the party to consist of half a dozen gentlemen and three ladies. They all started at the appointed hour except myself. I was at the Government Prison, and got so interested in its examination that I did not notice how quickly the time was passing. Somebody remarked that it was twenty minutes past five o'clock, and that woke me up. It was a fortunate circumstance that Captain Phillips was there with his 'turn-out,' as he calls a top-buggy that Captain Cook brought here in 1778, and a horse that was here when Captain Cook came. Captain Phillips takes a just pride in his driving and in the speed of his horse, and to his passion for displaying them I owe it that we were only sixteen minutes coming from the prison to the American Hotel—a distance which has been estimated to be over half a mile. But it took some awful driving. The Captain's whip came down fast, and the blows started so much dust out of the horse's hide that during the last half of the journey we rode through an impenetrable fog, and ran by a pocket compass in the hands of Captain Fish, a whaler captain of twenty-six years' experience, who sat there through that perilous voyage as self-possessed as if he had been on the euchre-deck of his own ship, and calmly said, 'Port your helm—port,' from time to time, and 'Hold her a little free—steady—so-o,' and 'Luff—hard down to starboard!' and never once lost his presence of mind or betrayed the least anxiety by voice or manner. When we came to anchor at last, and Captain Phillips looked at his watch and said, 'Sixteen minutes—I told you it was in her! that 's over three miles an hour!' I could see he felt entitled to a compliment, so I said I had never seen lightning go like that horse. And I never had.

The landlord of the American said the party had been gone nearly an hour, but that he could give me my choice of several horses that could easily overtake them. I said, never mind—I preferred a safe horse to a fast one—I would like to have an excessively gentle horse—a horse with no spirit whatever—a lame one, if he had such a thing. Inside of five minutes I was mounted, and perfectly satisfied with my outfit. I had no time to label him 'This is a horse,' and so if the public took him for a sheep I cannot help it. I was satisfied, and that was the main thing. I could see that he had as many fine points as any man's horse, and I just hung my hat on one of them, behind the saddle, and swabbed the perspiration from my face and started. I named him after this island, 'Oahu' (pronounced O-wa-hoo). The first gate he came to he started in; I had neither whip nor spur, and so I simply argued the case with him. He firmly resisted argument, but ultimately yielded to insult and abuse. He backed out of the gate and steered for another one on the other side of the street. I triumphed by my former process. Within the next six hundred yards he crossed the street fourteen times and attempted thirteen gates, and in the meantime the tropical sun was beating down and threatening to cave the top of my head in, and I was literally dripping with perspiration and profanity. (I am only human and I was sorely aggravated. I shall behave better next time.) He quit the gate business after that and went along peaceably enough, but absorbed in meditation. I noticed this latter circumstance, and it soon began to fill me with the gravest apprehension. I said to myself, this malignant brute is planning some new outrage, some fresh deviltry or other —no horse ever thought over a subject so profoundly as this one is doing just for nothing. The more this thing preyed upon my mind the more uneasy I became, until at last the suspense became unbearable and I dismounted to see if there was anything wild in his eye—for I had heard that the eye of this noblest of our domestic animals is very expressive. I cannot describe what a load of anxiety was lifted from my mind when I found that he was only asleep. I woke him up and started him into a faster walk, and then the inborn villainy of his nature came out again. He tried to climb over a stone wall, five or six feet high. I saw that I must apply force to this horse, and that

I might as well begin first as last. I plucked a stout switch from a tamarind tree, and the moment he saw it, he gave in. He broke into a convulsive sort of a canter, which had three short steps in it and one long one, and reminded me alternately of the clattering shake of the great earthquake, and the sweeping plunging of the *Ajax* in a storm.

And now it occurs to me that there can be no fitter occasion than the present to pronounce a fervent curse upon the man who invented the American saddle. There is no seat to speak of about it—one might as well sit in a shovel—and the stirrups are nothing but an ornamental nuisance. If I were to write down here all the abuse I expended on those stirrups, it would make a large book, even without pictures. Sometimes I got one foot so far through that the stirrup partook of the nature of an anklet; sometimes both feet were through, and I was handcuffed by the legs, and sometimes my feet got clear out and left the stirrups wildly dangling about my shins. Even when I was in proper position and carefully balanced upon the balls of my feet, there was no comfort in it, on account of my nervous dread that they were going to slip one way or the other in a moment. But the subject is too exasperating to write about.

This is a good time to drop in a paragraph of information. There is no regular livery stable in Honolulu, or, indeed, in any part of the kingdom of Hawaii; therefore, unless you are acquainted with wealthy residents (who all have good horses), you must hire animals of the vilest description from the Kanakas. Any horse you hire, even though it be from a white man, is not often of much account, because it will be brought in for you from some ranch, and has necessarily been leading a hard life. If the Kanakas who have been caring for him (inveterate riders they are) have not ridden him half to death every day themselves, you can depend upon it they have been doing the same thing by proxy, by clandestinely hiring him out. At least, so I am informed. The result is, that no horse has a chance to eat, drink, rest, recuperate, or look well or feel well, and so strangers go about the islands mounted as I was to-day.

In hiring a horse from a Kanaka, you must have all your eyes about you, because you can rest satisfied that you are dealing with as shrewd a rascal as ever patronized a penitentiary. You may leave your door open and your trunk unlocked as long as you please, and he will not meddle with your property; he has no important vices and no inclination to commit robbery on a large scale; but if he can get ahead of you in the horse business, he will take a genuine delight in doing it. This trait is characteristic of horse jockeys the world over, is it not? He will overcharge you if he can; he will hire you a fine-looking horse at night (anybody's—maybe the King's, if the royal steed be in convenient view), and bring you the mate to my Oahu in the morning, and contend that it is the same animal. If you raise a row, he will get out by saying it was not himself who made the bargain with you, but his brother, 'who went out in the country this morning.' They have always got a 'brother' to shift the responsibility upon. A victim said to one of these fellows one day:

'But I know I hired the horse of you, because I noticed that scar on your cheek.'

The reply was not bad: 'Oh, yes—yes—my brother all same—we twins!'

A friend of mine, J. Smith, hired a horse yesterday, the Kanaka warranting him to be in excellent condition. Smith had a saddle and blanket of his own, and he ordered the Kanaka to put these on the horse. The Kanaka protested that he was perfectly willing to trust the gentleman with the saddle that was already on the animal, but Smith refused to use it. The change was made; then Smith noticed that the Kanaka had changed only the saddles, and had left the original blanket on the horse; he said he forgot to change the blankets, and so, to cut the bother short, Smith mounted and rode away. The horse went lame a mile from town, and afterward got to cutting up some extraordinary capers. Smith got down and took off the saddle, but the blanket stuck fast to the horse—glued to a procession of raw sores. The Kanaka's mysterious conduct stood explained.

Another friend of mine bought a pretty good horse from a native, a day or two ago, after a tolerably thorough examination of the animal. He discovered to-day that the horse was as blind as a bat, in one eye. He meant to have examined that eye, and came home with a general notion that he had done it; but he remembers now that every time he made the attempt his attention was called to something else by his victimizer.

One more yarn, and then I will pass to something else. I am informed that when Leland was here he bought a pair of very respectable-looking match horses from a native. They were in a little stable with a partition through the middle of it—one horse in each apartment. Leland examined one of them critically through a window (the Kanaka's 'brother' having gone to the country with the key), and then went around the house and examined the other through a window on the other side. He said it was the neatest match he had ever seen, and paid for the horses on the spot. Whereupon the Kanaka departed to join his brother in the country. The scoundrel had shamefully swindled Leland. There was only one 'match' horse, and he had examined his starboard side through one window and his port side through another! I decline to believe this story, but I give it because it is worth something as a fanciful illustration of a fixed fact—namely, that the Kanaka horse-jockey is fertile in invention and elastic in conscience.

You can buy a pretty good horse for forty or fifty dollars, and a good enough horse for all practical purposes for two dollars and a half. I estimate Oahu to be worth somewhere in the neighborhood of thirty-five cents. A good deal better animal than he is was sold here day before yesterday for a dollar and six bits, and sold again to-day for two dollars and twenty-five cents; Brown bought a handsome and lively little pony yesterday for ten dollars; and about the best common horse on the island (and he is a really good one) sold yesterday, with good Mexican saddle and bridle, for seventy dollars—a horse which is well and widely known, and greatly respected for his speed, good disposition and everlasting bottom. You give your horse a little grain once a day; it comes from San Francisco, and is worth about two cents a pound; and you give him as much hay as he wants; it is cut and brought to the market by natives, and is not very good; it is baled into long, round bundles, about the size of a large man; one of them is stuck by the middle on each end of a six-foot pole, and the Kanaka shoulders the pole and walks about the streets between the upright bales in search of customers. These hay bales, thus carried, have a general resemblance to a colossal capital H.

The hay-bundles cost twenty-five cents apiece, and one will last a horse about a day. You can get a horse for a song, a week's hay for another song, and you can turn your animal loose among the luxuriant grass in your neighbor's broad front yard without a song at all—you do it at midnight, and stable the beast again before morning. You have been at no expense thus far, but when you come to buy a saddle and bridle they will cost you from $20 to $35. You can hire a horse, saddle and bridle at from $7 to $10 a week, and the owner will take care of them at his own expense.

Well, Oahu worried along over a smooth, hard road, bordered on either side by cottages, at intervals, pulu swamps at intervals, fish ponds at intervals, but through a dead level country all the time, and no trees to hide the wide Pacific Ocean on the right or the rugged, towering rampart of solid rock, called Diamond Head or Diamond Point, straight ahead.

A mile and a half from town, I came to a grove of tall cocoanut trees, with clean, branchless stems reaching straight up sixty or seventy feet and topped with a spray of green foliage sheltering clusters of cocoa-nuts—not more picturesque than a forest of colossal ragged parasols, with bunches of magnified grapes under them, would be. About a dozen cottages, some frame and the others of native grass, nestled sleepily in the shade here and there. The grass cabins are of a grayish color, are shaped much like our own cottages, only with higher and steeper roofs usually, and are made of some kind of weed strongly bound together in bundles. The roofs are very thick, and so are the walls; the latter have square holes in them for windows. At a little distance these cabins have a furry appearance, as if they might be made of bear skins. They are very cool and pleasant inside. The King's flag was flying from the roof of one of the cottages, and His Majesty was probably within. He owns the whole concern thereabouts, and passes his time there frequently, on sultry days 'laying off.' The spot is called 'The King's Grove.'

Nearby is an interesting ruin—the meager remains of an ancient heathen temple—a place where human sacricfies were offered up in those old bygone days when the simple child of nature, yielding momentarily to sin when sorely tempted, acknowledged his error when calm reflection had shown it to him, and came forward with noble frankness and offered up his grandmother as an atoning sacrifice—in those old days when the luckless sinner could keep on cleansing his conscience and achieving periodical happiness as long as his relations held out; long, long before the missionaries braved a thousand privations to come and make them permanently miserable by telling them how beautiful and how blissful a place heaven is, and how nearly impossible it is to get there; and showed the poor native how dreary a place perdition is and what unnecessarily liberal facilities there are for going to it; showed him how, in his ignorance, he had gone and fooled away all his kin-folks to no purpose; showed him what rapture it is to work all day long for fifty cents to buy food for next day with, as compared with fishing for pastime and lolling in the shade through eternal Summer, and eating of the bounty that nobody labored to provide but Nature. How sad it is to think of the multitudes who have gone to their graves in this beautiful island and never knew there was a hell! And it inclines right thinking man to weep rather than to laugh when he reflects how surprised they must have been when they got there. This ancient temple was built of rough blocks of lava, and was simply a roofless inclosure a hundred and thirty feet long and seventy wide—nothing but naked walls, very thick, but not much higher than a man's head. They will last for ages, no doubt, if left unmolested. Its three altars and other sacred appurtenances have crumbled and passed away years ago. It is said that in the old times thousands of human beings were slaughtered here, in the presence of multitudes of naked, whooping and howling savages. If these mute stones could speak, what tales they could tell, what pictures they could describe, of fettered victims, writhing and shrieking under the knife; of dense masses of dusky forms straining forward out of the gloom, with eager and ferocious faces lit up with the weird light of sacrificial fires; of the vague background of ghostly trees; of the mournful sea washing the dim shore; of the dark pyramid of Diamond Head standing sentinel over the dismal scene, and the peaceful moon looking calmly down upon it through rifts in the drifting clouds!

When Kamehameha (pronounced Ka-may-ah-may-ah) the Great—who was a very Napoleon in military genius and uniform success—invaded this island of Oahu three-quarters of a century ago, and exterminated the army sent to oppose him, and took full and final possession of the country, he searched out the dead body of the king of Oahu, and those of the principal chiefs, and impaled their heads upon the walls of this temple.

Those were savage times when this old slaughter-house was in its prime. The king and the chiefs ruled the common herd with a rod of iron; made them gather all the provisions the masters needed; build all the houses and temples; stand all the expenses, of whatever kind; take kicks and cuffs for thanks; drag out lives well flavored with misery, and then suffer death for trifling offenses or yield up their lives on the sacrificial altars to purchase favors from the gods for their hard rulers. The missionaries have clothed them, educated them, broken up the tyrannous authority of their chiefs, and given them freedom and the right to enjoy whatever the labor of their hand and brain produces, with equal laws for all and punishment for all alike who transgress them. The contrast is so strong—the wonderful benefit conferred upon this people by the missionaries is so prominent, so palpable and so unquestionable, that the frankest compliment I can pay them, and the best, is simply to point to the condition of the Sandwich Islanders of Captain Cook's time, and their condition to-day. Their work speaks for itself.

The little collection of cottages (of which I was speaking a while ago) under the cocoanut trees is an historical point. It is the village of Waikiki (usually pronounced Wy-kee-ky), once the capital of the kingdom and the abode of the great Kamehameha I. In 1801, while he lay encamped at this place with seven thousand men, preparing to invade the island of Kaui (he had previously captured and subdued the seven other inhabited islands of the group, one after another), a pestilence broke out in Oahu and raged with great virulence. It attacked the king's army and made great havoc in it. It is said that three hundred bodies were washed out to sea in one day.

There is an opening in the coral reef at this point, and anchorage inside for a small number of vessels, though one accustomed to the great Bay of San Francisco would never take this little belt of smooth water, with its border of foaming surf, to be a harbor, save for Whitehall boats or something of that kind. But harbors are scarce in the islands—open roadsteads are the rule here. The harbor of Waikiki was discovered in 1786 (seven or eight years after Captain Cook's murder) by Captain Portlock and Dixon, in the ships *King George* and *Queen Charlotte* —the first English vessels that visited the islands after that unhappy occurrence. This little bathing tub of smooth water possesses some further historical interest as being the spot where the distinguished navigator, Vancouver, landed when he came here in 1792.

In a conversation with a gentleman to-day about the scarcity of harbors among the islands (and in all the islands of the South Pacific), he said the natives of Tahiti have a theory that the reason why there are harbors wherever fresh water streams empty into the sea, and none elsewhere, is that fresh water kills the coral insect, or so discommodes or disgusts it that it will not build its stony wall in its vicinity, and instance what is claimed as fact, viz, that the break in the reef is always found where the fresh water passes over it, in support of this theory. (This notable equestrian excursion will be concluded in my next, if nothing happens.)

Mark Twain

Reprinted from the Sacramento Weekly Union
April 28, 1866.

THE ISLAND BY NIGHT

March — 1866.

I WANDERED along the sea beach on my steed Oahu around the base of the extinct crater of Leahi, or Diamond Head, and a quarter of a mile beyond the point I overtook the party of ladies and gentlemen and assumed my proper place—that is, in the rear—for the horse I ride always persists in remaining in the rear in spite of kicks, cuffs and curses. I was satisfied as long as I could keep Oahu within hailing distance of the cavalcade—I knew I could accomplish nothing better even if Oahu were Norfolk himself.

We went on—on—on—a great deal too far, I thought, for people who were unaccustomed to riding on horseback, and who must expect to suffer on the morrow if they indulged too freely in this sort of exercise. Finally we got to a point which we were expecting to go around in order to strike an easy road home; but we were too late; it was full tide and the sea had closed in on the shore. Young Henry McFarlane said he knew a nice, comfortable route over the hill—a short cut—and the crowd dropped into his wake. We climbed a hill a hundred and fifty feet high, and about as straight up and down as the side of a house, and as full of rough lava blocks as it could stick—not as wide, perhaps, as the broad road that leads to destruction, but nearly as dangerous to travel, and apparently leading in the same general direction. I felt for the ladies, but I had no time to speak any words of sympathy, by reason of my attention being so much occupied by Oahu. The place was so steep that at times he stood straight up on his tip-toes and clung by his forward toe-nails, with his back to the Pacific Ocean and his nose close to the moon—and thus situated we formed an equestrian picture which was as uncomfortable to me as it may have been picturesque to the spectators. You may think I was afraid, but I was not. I knew I could stay on him as long as his ears did not pull out.

It was great relief to me to know that we were all safe and sound on the summit at last, because the sun was just disappearing in the waves, night was abroad in the land, candles and lamps were already twinkling in the distant town, and we gratefully reflected that Henry had saved us from having to go back around that rocky, sandy beach. But a new trouble arose while the party were admiring the rising moon and the cool, balmy night-breeze, with its odor of countless flowers, for it was discovered that we had got into a place we could not get out of—we were apparently surrounded by precipices—our pilot's chart was at fault, and he could not extricate us, and so we had the prospect before us of either spending the night in the admired night-breeze, under the admired moon, or of clambering down the way we came, in the dark. However, a Kanaka came along presently and found a first-rate road for us down an almost imperceptible decline, and the party set out on a cheerful gallop again, and Oahu struck up his miraculous canter once more.

The moon rose up, and flooded mountain and valley and ocean with silvery light, and I was not sorry we had lately been in trouble, because the consciousness of being safe again raised our spirits, and made us more capable of enjoying the beautiful scene than we would have been otherwise. I never breathed such a soft, delicious atmosphere before, nor one freighted with such rich fragrance. A barber shop is nothing to it.

Gayly laughing and talking, the party galloped on, and with set teeth and bouncing body I clung to the pommel and cantered after. Presently we came to a place where no grass grew—a wide expanse of deep sand. They said it was an old battle-ground. All around everywhere, not three feet apart, the bleached bones of men gleamed white in the moonlight. We picked up a lot of them for mementoes. I got quite a number of arm bones and leg bones—of great chiefs, maybe, who had fought savagely in that fearful battle in the old days, when blood flowed like wine where we now stood—and wore the choicest of them out on Oahu afterward, trying to make him go. All sorts of bones could be found except skulls; but a citizen said, irreverently, that there had been an unusual number of 'skull-hunters' there lately—a species of sportsmen I had never heard of before. The conversation at this point took a unique and ghastly turn. A gentleman said:

'Give me some of your bones, Miss Blank; I'll carry them for you.'

Another said:

'You haven't got bones enough, Mrs. Blank; here's a good shin-bone, if you want it.'

Such observations as these fell from the lips of ladies with reference to their queer newly-acquired property:

'Mr. Brown, will you please hold some of my bones for me a minute?' And,

'Mr. Smith, you have got some of my bones; and you have got one, too, Mr. Jones; and you have got my spine, Mr. Twain. Now don't any of you gentlemen get my bones all mixed up with yours so that you can't tell them apart.'

These remarks look very irreverent on paper, but they did not sound so, being used merely in a business way and with no intention of making sport of the remains. I did not think it was just right to carry off any of these bones, but we did it anyhow. We considered that it was at least as right as it is for the Hawaiian Government and the city of Honolulu (which is the most excessively moral and religious town that can be found on the map of the world), to permit those remains to lie decade after decade, to bleach and rot in sun and wind and suffer desecration by careless strangers and by the beasts of the field, unprotected by even a worm-fence. Call us hard names if you will, you statesmen and missionaries! but I say shame upon you, that after raising a nation from idolatry to Chistianity, and from barbarism to civilization, you have not taught it the comment of respect for the dead. Your work is incomplete.

Nothing whatever is known about this place—its story is a secret that will never be revealed. The oldest natives make no pretense of being possessed of its history. They say these bones were here when they were children. They were here when their grandfathers were children—but how they came here, they can only conjecture. Many people believe this spot to be an ancient battle-ground, and it is usual to call it so; and they believe that these skeletons have lain for ages just where their proprietors fell in the great fight. Other people believe that Kamehameha I fought his first battle here. On this point, I have heard a story, which may have been taken from one of the numerous books which have been written concerning these islands—I do not know where the narrator got it. He said that when Kamehameha (who was at first merely a subordinate chief on the island of Hawaii), landed here, he brought a large army with him, and encamped at Waikiki. The Oahuans marched against him, and so confident were they of success that they readily acceded to a demand of their priests that they should draw a line where these bones now lie, and take an oath that, if forced to retreat at all, they would never retreat beyond this boundary. The priests told them that death and ever-lasting punishment would overtake any who violated the oath, and the march was resumed. Kamehameha drove them back step by step; the priests fought in the front rank and exhorted them both by voice and inspiriting example to remember their oath—to die, if need be, but never cross the fatal line. The struggle was manfully maintained, but at last the chief priest fell, pierced to the heart with a spear, and the unlucky omen fell like a blight upon the brave souls at his back; with a triumphant shout the invaders pressed forward—the line was crossed—the offended gods deserted the despairing army, and, accepting the doom their perjury had brought upon them, they broke and fled over the plain where Honolulu stands now—up the beautiful Nuuanu Valley—paused a moment, hemmed in by precipitous mountains on either hand and the frightful precipice of the Pari (pronounced *Pally*; intelligent natives claim that there is no *r* in in the Kanaka alphabet) in front, and then were driven over—a sheer plunge of six hundred feet!

The story is pretty enough, but Mr. Jarves' excellent history says the Oahuans were intrenched in Nuuanu Valley; that Kamehameha ousted them, routed them, pursued them up the valley and drove them over the precipice. He makes no mention of our bone-yard at all in his book.

There was a terrible pestilence here in 1804 which killed great numbers of the inhabitants, and the natives have legends of others that swept the islands long before that; and therefore many persons now believe that these bones belonged to victims of one of these epidemics who were hastily buried in a great pit. It is by far the most reasonable conjecture, because Jarves says that the weapons of the Islanders were so rude and inefficient that their battles were not often very bloody. If this was a battle it was astonishingly deadly, for in spite of the depredations of 'skull hunters,' we rode a considerable distance over ground so thickly strewn with human bones that the horses' feet crushed them, not occasionally, but at every step.

Impressed by the profound silence and repose that rested over the beautiful landscape, and being, as usual, in the rear, I gave voice to my thoughts. I said:

'What a picture is here slumbering in the solemn glory of the moon! How strong the rugged outlines of the dead volcano stand out against the clear sky! What a snowy fringe marks the bursting of the surf over the long, curved reef! How calmly the dim city sleeps yonder in the plain! How soft the shadows lie upon the stately mountains that border the dream-haunted Manoa Valley! What a grand pyramid of billowy clouds towers above the storied Pari! How the grim warriors of the past seem flocking in ghostly squadrons to their ancient battlefield again—how the wails of the dying well up from the—'

At this point the horse called Oahu deliberately sat down in the sand. Sat down to listen, I suppose. Never mind what he heard. I stopped apostrophising and convinced him that I was not a man to allow Contempt of Court on the part of a horse. I broke the back-bone of a chief over his rump and set out to join the cavalcade again.

Very considerably fagged out we arrived in town at 9 o'clock at night, myself in the lead—for when my horse finally came to understand that he was homeward bound and hadn't far to go, he threw his legs wildly out before and behind him, depressed his head and laid his ears back, and flew by the admiring company like a telegram. In five minutes he was far away ahead of everybody.

We stopped in front of a private residence — Brown and I did — to wait for the rest and see that none were lost. I soon saw that I had attracted the attention of a comely young girl, and I felt duly flattered. Perhaps, thought I, she admires my horsemanship — and I made a savage jerk at the bridle and said, 'Ho! will you!' to show how fierce and unmanageable the beast was — though, to say truly, he was leaning up against a hitching-post peaceably enough at the time. I stirred Oahu up and moved him about, and went up the street a short distance to look for the party, and 'loped' gallantly back again, all the while making a pretense of being unconscious that I was an object of interest. I then addressed a few 'peart' remarks to Brown, to give the young lady a chance to admire my style of conversation, and was gratified to see her step up and whisper to Brown and glance furtively at me at the same time. I could see that her gentle face bore an expression of the most kindly and earnest solicitude, and I was shocked and angered to hear Brown burst into a fit of brutal laughter.

As soon as we started home, I asked, with a fair show of indifference, what she had been saying.

Brown laughed again and said: 'She thought from the slouchy way you rode and the way you drawled out your words, that you was drunk! She said, "Why don't you take the poor creature home, Mr. Brown? It makes me nervous to see him galloping that horse and just hanging on that way, and he so drunk." '

I laughed very loudly at the joke, but it was a sort of hollow, sepulchral laugh, after all. And then I took it out of Oahu.

I have found an old acquaintance here — Rev. Franklin S. Rising, of the Episcopal ministry, who has had charge of a church in Virginia, Nevada, for several years, and who is well known in Sacramento and San Francisco. He sprained his knee in September last, and is here for his health. He thinks he has made no progress worth mentioning towards regaining it, but I think differently. He can ride on horseback, and is able to walk a few steps without his crutches—things he could not do a week ago.

The popular-song nuisance follows us here. In San Francisco it used to be 'Just Before the Battle Mother,' every night and all night long. Then it was 'When Johnny Comes Marching Home.' After that it was 'Wearin' of the Green.' And last and most dreadful of all, came that calamity of 'When We Were Marching Through Georgia.' It was the last thing I heard when the ship sailed, and it gratified me to think I should hear it no more for months. And now, here at dead of night, at the very outpost and fag-end of the world, on a little rock in the middle of a limitless ocean, a pack of dark-skinned savages are tramping down the street singing it with a vim and energy that make my hair rise!—singing it in their own barbarous tongue! They have got the tune to perfection—otherwise I never would have suspected that

Waikiki lantani œ Kaa hooly hooly wawhoo

means 'When We Were Marching Through Georgia.' If it would have been all the same to General Sherman, I wish he had gone around by the way of the Gulf of Mexico, instead of marching through Georgia.

MARK TWAIN

Reprinted from the Sacramento Weekly Union
April 28, 1866.

SATURDAY IN HONOLULU

April — 1866.

MOUNTED on my noble steed Hawaii (pronounced Hah-wy-ye—stress on second syllable), a beast that cost thirteen dollars and is able to go his mile in three—with a bit of margin to it—I departed last Saturday week for—any place that might turn up.

Passing through the market place we saw that feature of Honolulu under its most favorable auspices—that is, in the full glory of Saturday afternoon, which is a festive day with the natives. The native girls by twos and threes and parties of a dozen, and sometimes in whole platoons and companies, went cantering up and down the neighboring streets astride of fleet but homely horses, and with their gaudy riding habits streaming like banners behind them. Such a troop of free and easy riders, in their natural home, which is the saddle, makes a gay and graceful and exhilarating spectacle. The riding habit I speak of is simply a long, broad scarf, like a tavern table cloth brilliantly colored, wrapped around the loins once, then apparently passed up between the limbs and each end thrown backward over the same, and floating and flapping behind on both sides beyond the horse's tail like a couple of fancy flags; and then, with a girl that throws her chest forward and sits up like a Major-General and goes sweeping by like the wind. 'Gay?' says Brown, with a fine irony; 'oh, you can't mean it!'

The girls put on all the finery they can scare up on Saturday afternoon — fine black silk robes; flowing red ones that nearly put your eyes out; others as white as snow; still others that discount the rainbow; and they wear their hair in nets, and trim their jaunty hats with fresh flowers, and encircle their dusky throats with home-made necklaces of the brilliant vermillion-tinted blossom of the *ohia*; and they fill the markets and the adjacent streets with their bright presences, and smell like thunder with their villainous cocoa-nut oil.

Occasionally you see a heathen from the sunny isles away down in the South Seas, with his face and neck tattooed till he looks like the customary unfortunate from Reese River who has been blown up in a mine. Some are tattooed a dead blue color down to the upper lip—masked, as it were—leaving the natural light yellow skin of Micronesia unstained from thence down; some with broad marks drawn down from hair to neck, on both sides of the face, and a strip of the original yellow skin, two inches wide, down the center—a gridiron with a spoke broken out; and some with the entire face discolored with the popular mortification tint, relieved only by one or two thin, wavy threads of natural yellow running across the face from ear to ear, and eyes twinkling out of this darkness, from under shadowing hat-brims, like stars in the dark of the moon.

Moving among the stirring crowds, you come to the poi merchants, squatting in the shade on their hams, in true native fashion, and surrounded by purchasers. (The Sandwich Islanders always squat on their hams, and who knows but they may be the old original 'ham sandwiches?' The thought is pregnant with interest.) The poi looks like common flour paste, and is kept in large bowls formed of a species of gourd, and capable of holding from one to three or four gallons. Poi is the chief article of food among the natives, and is prepared from the *kalo* or *taro* plant (*k* and *t* are the same in the Kanaka alphabet, and so are *l* and *r*). The taro root looks like a thick, or, if you please, a corpulent sweet potato, in shape, but is of a light purple color when boiled. When boiled it answers as a passable substitute for bread. The buck Kanakas bake it under ground, then mash it up well with a heavy lava pestle, mix water with it until it becomes a paste, set it aside and let it ferment, and then it is poi —and a villainous mixture it is, almost tasteless before it ferments and too sour for a luxury afterward. But nothing in the world is more nutritious. When solely used, however, it produces acrid humors, a fact which sufficiently accounts for the blithe and humorous character of the Kanakas. I think there must be as much of a knack in handling poi as there is in eating with chopsticks. The forefinger is thrust into the mess and stirred quickly round several times and drawn as quickly out, thickly coated, just as if it were poulticed; the head is thrown back, the finger inserted in the mouth and the poultice stripped off and swallowed—the eye closing gently, meanwhile, in a languid sort of ecstasy. Many a different finger goes into the same bowl and many a different kind of dirt and shade and quality of flavor is added to the virtues of its contents. One tall gentleman, with nothing in the world on but a soiled and greasy shirt, thrust in his finger and tested the poi, shook his head, scratched it with the useful finger, made another test, prospected among his hair, caught something and eat it; tested the poi again, wiped the grimy perspiration from his brow with the universal hand, tested again, blew his nose—'Let's move on, Brown,' said I, and we moved.

Around a small shanty was collected a crowd of natives buy-the *awa* root. It is said that but for the use of this root the destruction of the people in former times by venereal diseases would have been far greater than it was, and by others it is said that this is merely a fancy. All agree that poi will rejuvenate a man who is used up and his vitality almost annihilated by hard drinking, and that in some kinds of diseases it will restore health after all medicines have failed; but all are not willing to allow to the *awa* the virtues claimed for it. The natives manufacture an intoxicating drink from it which is fearful in its effects when persistently indulged in. It covers the body with dry, white scales, inflames the eyes, and causes premature decrepitude. Although the man before whose establishment we stopped has to pay a Government license of eight hundred dollars a year for an exclusive right to sell *awa* root, it is said that he makes a small fortune every twelvemonth; while saloon keepers, who pay a thousand dollars a year for the privilege of retailing whisky, etc., only make a bare living.

We found the fish market crowded; for the native is very fond of fish, and eats the article raw. Let us change the subject.

In old times here Saturday was a grand gala day indeed. All the native population of the town forsook their labors, and those of the surrounding country journeyed to the city. Then the white folks had to stay indoors, for every street was so packed with charging cavaliers and cavalieresses that it was next to impossible to thread one's way through the cavalcades without getting crippled. In the afternoon the natives were wont to repair to the plain, outside the town, and indulge in their ancient sports and pastimes and bet away their week's earnings on horse races. One might see two or three thousand, some say five thousand, of these wild riders, skurrying over the plain in a mass in those days. And it must have been a fine sight.

At night they feasted and the girls danced the lascivious *hula hula*—a dance that is said to exhibit the very perfection of educated motion of limb and arm, hand, head and body, and the exactest uniformity of movement and accuracy of 'time.' It was performed by a circle of girls with no raiment on them to speak of, who went through with an infinite variety of motions and figures without prompting, and yet so true was their 'time,' and in such perfect concert did they move that when they were placed in a straight line, hands, arms, bodies, limbs and heads waved, swayed, gesticulated, bowed, stooped, whirled, squirmed, twisted and undulated as if they were part and parcel of a single individual; and it was difficult to believe they were not moved in a body by some exquisite piece of mechanism.

Of late years, however, Saturday has lost most of its quondam gala features. This weekly stampede of the natives interfered too much with labor and the interests of the white folks, and by sticking in a law here, and preaching a sermon there, and by various other means, they gradually broke it up. The demoralizing *hula hula* was forbidden to be performed, save at night, with closed doors, in the presence of a few spectators, and only by permission duly procured from the authorities and the payment of ten dollars for the same. There are few girls now-a-days able to dance this ancient national dance in the highest perfection of the art.

Cantering across the bridge and down the firm, level, gleaming white coral turnpike that leads toward the south, or the east, or the west, or the north (the points of the compass being all the same to me, inasmuch as, for good reasons, I have not had an opportunity thus far of discovering whereabouts the sun rises in this country—I know where it sets, but I don't know how it gets there nor which direction it comes from), we presently arrived at a massive coral edifice which I took for a fortress at first, but found out directly that it was the Government prison. A soldier at the great gate admitted us without further authority than my countenance, and I suppose he thought he was paying me a handsome compliment when he did so; and so did I until I reflected that the place was a penitentiary. However, as far as appearances went, it might have been the King's palace, so neat, and clean, and white, and so full of the fragrance of flowers was the establishment, and I was satisfied.

We passed through a commodious office whose walls were ornamented with linked strands of polished handcuffs and fetters, through a hall, and among the cells above and below. The cells for the men were eight or ten feet high, and roomy enough to accommodate the two prisoners and their hammocks, usually put in each, and have space left for several more. The floors were scrubbed clean, and were guiltless of spot or stain of any kind, and the painfully white walls were unmarred by a single mark or blemish. Through ample gratings, one could see the blue sky and get his hair blown off by the cool breeze. They call this a prison—the pleasantest quarters in Honolulu.

There are four wards, and one hundred and thirty-two prisoners can be housed in rare and roomy comfort within them.

There were a number of native women in the female department. Poor devils, they hung their heads under the prying eyes of our party as if they were really ashamed of being there.

In the condemned cell and squatting on the floor, all swathed in blankets, as if it were cold weather, was a brown-faced, gray-bearded old scaliwag, who, in a frolicsome mood, had massacred three women and a batch of children—his own property, I believe—and reflects upon that exploit with genuine satisfaction to this hour, and will go to the gallows as tranquilly indifferent as a white man would go to dinner.

The prison-yard—that sad inclosure which, in the prisons of my native America, is a cheerless barren and yieldeth no vegetation save the gallows-tree, with its sorrowful human fruit—is a very garden! The beds, bordered by rows of inverted bottles (the usual style here), were filled with all manner of dainty flowers and shrubs; Chinese mulberry and orange trees stood here and there, well stocked with fruit; a beautiful little pine tree—rare, and imported from the South Seas—occupied the center, with sprays of gracefully arching green spears springing outward like parasol tops, at marked and regular intervals, up its slender stem, and diminishing in diameter with mathematical strictness of graduation, till the sprouting plume at the top stood over a perfect pyramid. Vines clambered everywhere and hid from view and clothed with beauty everything that might otherwise have been suggestive of chains and captivity. There was nothing here to remind one of the prison save a brace of dovecotes, containing several pretty birds brought hither from 'strange, strange lands beyond the sea.' These, sometimes, may pine for liberty and their old free life among the clouds or in the shade of the orange groves, or abroad on the breezy ocean—but if they do, it is likely they take it out in pining, as a general thing.

Against one wall of the prison house stands an airy little building which does duty as a hospital. A harmless old lunatic, named Captain Tait, has his quarters here. He has a wife and children in the town, but he prefers the prison hospital, and has demanded and enjoyed its hospitality (slip of the pen—no joke intended) for years. He visits his family at long intervals—being free to go and come as he pleases—but he always drifts back to the prison again after a few days. His is a religious mania, and he professes to read sixty chapters of the Bible every day, and write them down in a book. He was about down to chapter thirty-five when I was introduced to him, I should judge, as it was nearly two in the afternoon.

I said, 'What book are you reading, Captain?'

'The precious of the precious—the book of books—the Sacred Scriptures, sir.'

'Do you read a good deal in it?'

'Sixty chapters every day' (with a perceptible show of vanity, but a weary look in the eye withal) '—sixty chapters every day, and write them all down in a plain, legible hand.'

'It is a good deal. At that rate, you must ultimately get through, and run short of material.'

'Ah, but the Lord looks out for his own. I am in His hands—He does with me as He wills. I often read some of the same chapters over again, for the Lord tells me what to read, and it is not for me to choose. Providence always shows me the place.'

'No hanging fire?—I mean, can you always depend on—on this information coming to time every day, so to speak?'

'Always—always, sir. I take the sacred volume in my hand, in this manner, every morning, in a devout and prayerful spirit, and immediately, and without any volition on my part, my fingers insert themselves between the leaves—so directed from above' (with a sanctified glance aloft) '—and I know that the Lord desires me to open at that place and begin. I never have to select the chapter myself—the Lord always does it for me.'

I heard Brown mutter, 'The old man appears to have a good thing, anyway—and his poi don't cost him anything, either; Providence looks out for his regular sixty, the prison looks out for his hash, and his family looks out for itself. I've never see any sounder maniac than him, and I've been around considerable.'

We were next introduced to General George Washington, or, at least, to an aged, limping negro man, who called himself by that honored name. He was supposed to be seventy years old, and he looked it. He was as crazy as a loon, and sometimes, they say, he grows very violent. He was a Samson in a small way; his arms were corded with muscle, and his legs felt as hard as if they were made of wood. He was in a peaceable mood at present, and strongly manacled. They have a hard time with him occasionally, and some time or other he will get in a lively way and eat up the garrison of that prison, no doubt. The native soldiers who guard the place are afraid of him, and he knows it.

His history is a sealed book—or at least all that part of it which transpired previously to the entry of his name as a pensioner upon the Hawaiian Government fifteen years ago. He was found carrying on at a high rate at one of the other islands, and it is supposed he was put ashore there from a vessel called the *Olive Branch*. He has evidently been an old sailor, and it is thought he was one of a party of negroes who fitted out a ship and sailed from a New England port some twenty years ago. He is fond of talking in his dreamy, incoherent way, about the Blue Ridge in Virginia, and seems familiar with Richmond and Lynchburg. I do not think he is the old original General W.

Up stairs in the prison are the handsome apartments used by the officers of the establishment; also a museum of quaint and curious weapons of offense and defense, of all nations and all ages of the world.

The prison is to a great extent a self-supporting institution, through the labor of the convicts farmed out to load and unload ships and work on the highways, and I am not sure but that it supports itself and pays a surplus into the public treasury besides, but I have no note of this, and I seldom place implicit confidence in my memory in matters where figures and finance are concerned and have not been thought of for a fortnight. This Government Prison is in the hands of W. C. Parke, Marshal of the Kingdom, and he has small need to be ashamed of his management of it. Without wishing to betray too much knowledge of such matters, I should say that this is the model prison of the western half of the world, at any rate.

MARK TWAIN

Reprinted from the Sacramento Weekly Union
May 26, 1866.

MRS. JOLLOPSON'S 'GAM'

April— 1866.

I HAVE just met an estimable lady—Mrs. Captain Jollopson, whose husband (with her assistance) commands the whaling bark *Lucretia Wilkerson*—and she said:

'Oh, I've never *had* such a time of it! I'm clean out of luck, I do believe. The wind's been dead ahead with me all this day. It appears to me that I can't do no way but that it comes out wrong. First I turned out this morning and says I, "Here's a go—eight bells and no duff yet! I just know it's going to blow great guns for *me* to-day." And so it's come out. Start fair, sail fair; otherwise, just the reverse. Well, I hove on my dress and cleared for the market, and took the big basket, which I don't do when I'm alone, because I'm on the short lay when it comes to eating; but when the old man's in port, it's different, you know, and I go fixed when I recruit for him—never come back in ballast then, because he's on the long lay, and it's expensive too; you can depend on it, his leakage and shrinkage shows up on his home bills when he goes out of port, and it's all on account of recruiting, too—though he says it's on account of toggery for me, which is a likely yarn, when I can't even buy a set of new halyards for my bonnet but he growls, and what few slops I do have I've got to smuggle 'em; and yet, bless you, if we were to ship 'em the freight on mine wouldn't pay primage on his—but where was I? Oh, yes—I hove on my dress and hove down toward the market, and while I was laying off and on before the Post Office, here comes a ship-keeper round the corner three sheets in the wind and his dead-lights stove in, and I see by the way he was bulling that if he didn't sheer off and shorten sail he'd foul my larboard stuns'l-boom, which I had my basket on—because, you see, he'd been among his friends having a bit of a gam, and had got about one fid too much aboard, and his judgment had fetched away in the meantime, and so he steered bad, and was making latitude all the time when he ought to been making longitude, and here he was to wind'ard of me, but making so much leeway that—well, you see how it was. I backed off fast as I could, and sung out to him to port his helm, but it warn't no use; he'd everything drawing and I had considerable sternway, and he just struck me a little abaft the beam, and down I went, head on, and skunned my elbow!'

I said, 'Bless my life!'

And she said, 'Well you may say it! My! such a jolt! It started everything. It's worse'n being pulled! I shouldn't wonder if I'd have to be hove down—' and then she spread her hand alongside of her mouth and sung out, 'Susy, ahoy!' to another woman, who rounded to to wait for her, and the two fell off before the wind and sailed away together.

Translation

'Eight bells' stands for the closing of a watch—two to an hour, four hours to a watch, six watches in a day—on board ship.

'Duff' is Jack Tar's dessert—a sort of dough, with dried apples or something of the kind in it on extra occasions.

'Cleared' for the market—A ship 'clears' for her voyage when she takes out her papers at the Custom-house.

'Short lay' and 'long lay'—These phrases are confined to the whaling interest. Neither the officers nor men get any wages on a whale-ship, but receive, instead, a proportion of all the bone and oil taken; Jack usually gets about the one-hundred-and-twentieth part of all the 'catch' (or profits of the voyage), for his share, and this is called a 'long lay;' the Captain generally gets a tenth, twelfth or fourteenth, which is a 'short lay,' and the other officers in proportion. Some Captains also have perquisites besides their 'lay'—a dollar or more on every barrel of the 'catch,' over a certain number. The luckiest Captain of the lot made $50,000 last season. Very good for a few months' work. When a ship is ready to sail and must suddenly supply the place of some seaman who has fallen sick, candidates will take advantage of the circumstances and demand as short a 'lay' as a second mate's to ship as the last man and complete the crew. I am informed (but I do not believe it), that this is termed the 'Lay of the Last Minstrel.'

'Recruit'—The whaling voyage to the North Seas occupies about seven months; then the vessel returns to Honolulu, tranships her oil to the States, refits and goes over to the coast of California about November or December, to put in her idle time catching hump-back whales or devil-fish, returning here along in March and April to 'recruit'—that is, procure vegetables, and especially potatoes, which are a protective against scurvy, and give the men a few days' run on shore, and then off for the north again as early in the Spring as possible. Those vessels which do not consider the coast fishing profitable, because of the 'stoving' of boats by the savage hump-backs and the consequent loss of men and material, go to 'west'ard,' as they term going down to the line after sperm whales; and when they have finished this 'between season,' they go over and 'recruit' at Japan, and from thence proceed directly north.

'Leakage and Shrinkage'—When a whaler returns here with her cargo, the United States Consul estimates its probable value in the East, and buys the interests of the officers and men on behalf of the owners of the ship, and pays for the same in gold. To secure the ship-owner against loss, a bill of contingencies is brought against poor Jack by the Consul (leakage and shrinkage being among the items), which reduces the profits of his long voyage about one-half or two-thirds. For instance, take the case of the whaling bark —— last year. The Consul considered oil to be worth between one dollar and seventy-five cents and two dollars a gallon (in greenbacks) in the States; he put it down at one dollar and seventy-five cents to be on the safe side, and then reduced as follows:

First—Premium to be paid for money, and difference between gold and paper—so much. (Jack must be paid in gold.)

Second—An allowance of eight per cent, for probable leakage and shrinkage of the oil on its homeward voyage.

Third—Freight on the homeward voyage—paid by Jack.

Fourth—Interest and insurance on the cargo hence to the States—paid by Jack.

Fifth—Commission of the owner at home (2½ per cent) for selling the cargo—paid by Jack.

And after all these reductions, what do you suppose the Consul paid Jack for his one hundred and twentieth 'lay' in a cargo of oil worth over $1.75 a gallon at home? He paid him seventy-four cents a gallon. As a general thing, the ship-owner at home makes a princely profit out of this 'gouging' of the sailor-man; but instances have occurred—rarely, however—where the price set by the Consul here was so much above the real value of the oil at home, that all the gouging was not sufficient to save the ship-owner from loss.

'Home Bills'—It makes no difference how much money a sailor brings into port, he is soon head over heels in debt. In order to secure his services on a voyage, the ship is obliged to assume this indebtedness. The item is entered against Jack on the ship's books at the home port in the East as his 'home bill.' If the voyage proves lucky, the ship gets even on Jack's home bill by subtracting it from his 'lay;' but if she takes no oil she must pay the bill anyhow, and is 'out and injured,' of course. These 'home bills' are first assumed by one of the professional 'sharks' in New Bedford and New London who furnish crews to ships; say Jack owes fifty dollars; the shark enters his name for a voyage, assumes his debt, advances him a dollar or so for a farewell spree, and takes his note for $150; and the ship-owner agrees to cash it at the end of six months. Ships have left port responsible for $5,000 home bills, lost four or five men by desertion, been to great trouble and expense to supply other men, and then had no luck and failed to catch a single whale.

'Slops'—Improvident Jack is apt to leave port short of jackets, trowsers, shirts, tobacco, pipes, letter-paper, and so forth and so on. The ship takes a large quantity of these things along, and supplies them to him at extremely healthy prices, so that sometimes, after a long, unlucky voyage, no wages and heavy home bills and bills for 'slops,' Jack will return to port very considerably in debt to the ship, and the ship must stand the loss, for an unprofitable voyage squares all such accounts. In squaring up a voyage before the consul, the ship-captain piles up the slop bills as high as he can get them, though it does not put a single cent in his own pockets; he forgets, in his enthusiasm for his owner's interest, that while he is gouging Jack for the benefit of 'the firm,' the firm are gouging himself, and Jack too, by the system of Consular assessment I have mentioned above. The Captain says to the Consul:

'Put down three pair of boots on this man's slop bill.'

Jack—'But I didn't have but one pair, sir.'

Captain—'Belay! Don't talk back; you might have had 'em if you'd a wanted 'em. And put him down for eleven pair of socks.'

Jack—'But I only had two pair, sir.'

Captain—'Well,——it, is that any o' my fault? Warn't they there for anybody that wanted 'em? And set him down for two ream of letter-paper.'

Jack—'Why, I never writ a letter whilst I was gone, sir.'

Captain—'Hold your yop! Do you cal'late for me to be responsible for all your dam foolishness? You might have had four ream, if you'd wanted it. And set on ten per cent for other truck, which I don't recollect what it was.'

And so Jack is gouged by the Captain, for the owner's exclusive benefit, and both are fleeced by that same owner with strict impartiality. Perhaps the Captain's 'lay' will go East to be sold, and 'the firm' will sell at a dollar and a half and then report to him that the market had fallen and they only got a dollar for it. Thus ungrateful are they to the Captain who gouged the seaman on his 'slops' for their sole benefit.

'Primage'—This term obtains in most seaports. No man can tell now what gave it birth, for it is very ancient, and its origin is long ago forgotten. It is a tax of five per cent on a ship's freight bills, and in old times went to her Captain. In our day, however, it goes to the ship-owner with the other freight money (although it forms a separate item in the freight bill), or is turned over to the agent who procured a cargo for a vessel, as his commission. When you engage for the shipment of a lot of freight, you make no mention of this five per cent primage, but you perfectly understand that it will be added, and you must pay it; therefore, when you are ostensibly shipping at twenty cents, you are really shipping at twenty-one.

'Laying off and on'—A sailor phrase, sufficiently well understood by landsmen to need no explanation.

'Ship-keeper'—A man who stands guard on a whaler and takes care of the ship when the boats and the crew are off after whales.

'Bulling'—A term usually applied to the chafing of vessels together when riding at anchor in harbors subject to chopping swells. Some whalers say that one reason why they avoid San Francisco is that this 'bulling' process in our Bay is more damaging to their vessels, frequently, than a long voyage.

'Gam'—The whaleman's phrase for gossip—very common here.

'Fid'—The whaleman's term for our 'smile'—drink. A fid is an instrument which the sailor uses when he splices the main brace on board ship.

'Fetched away'—A nautical phrase signifying to break loose from fastenings in a storm—such as the fetching away of furniture, rigging, etc.

'Skunned'—After examining various authors I have discovered that this is a provincial distortion of our word 'skinned.'

'Pulled'—A term signifying the arraigning of a ship's officers before the Courts by the crew to answer for alleged cruelties practiced upon them on the high seas—such as the 'pulling' of captains and mates by the crews of the *Mercury*, the *White Swallow*, the *Great Republic*, etc., in the San Francisco Courts. Here is another reason why, out of the eighty-seven American whaleships that will fish in the North Seas this Summer, only about sixteen will venture to touch at San Francisco either going or coming: they find it safer and cheaper to rendezvous and procure supplies here, and save 4,200 miles extra sailing, than to start from, and return to, San Francisco and run the chance of getting 'pulled.' Honolulu would not amount to anything at all without her whaling trade, and so Jack cannot 'pull' his Captain here—no matter what his grievance was, he could not easily get it before these courts; the lawyer who ventured to take his case would stand a fair chance of being run out of town by the enraged community. But the whaler-man says, 'You drop into 'Frisco and great Neptune! your men 'll pull you before you get your anchor down—and there you are for three months, on expenses, waiting on them Courts; and they'll go in and swear to the infernalest pack of lies, and the jury'll believe every word of it, and the Judge'll read you a sermon that'll take the hair off your head, and then he'll take and jam you into a jail. Oh, no; it don't pay a whaleship to stop at San Francisco.'

'Hove down'—In ports where there are docks, damaged vessels are hauled out and 'hove down' on their sides when repairs to their bottoms are required.

By this time, if you will go back and read the first paragraphs of this letter you may be able to understand them.

Every section of our western hemisphere seems supplied with a system of technicalities, etiquette and slang, peculiar to itself. The above chapter is intended to give you a somewhat exaggerated idea of the technicalities of conversation in Honolulu—bred from the great whaling interest which centers here, and naturally infused into the vocabulary of the place. Your favorite California similes were bred from the technicalities of surface mining; those of Washoe come from the profound depths of the 'main lead,' and those of the Honolulian were born of whalebone, blubber and the traffic of the seas. Perhaps no single individual would use more than two or three of the nautical and whaling phrases I have quoted, in any one conversation, but you might hear all of them in the course of a week, if you talked with a good many people.

And etiquette varies according to one's surroundings. In the mining camps of California, when a friend tenders you a 'smile' or invites you to take a 'blister,' it is etiquette to say, 'Here's hoping your dirt'll pan out gay.' In Washoe, when you are requested to 'put in a blast,' or invited to take 'your regular pison,' etiquette admonishes you to touch glasses and say, 'Here's hoping you'll strike it rich in the lower level.' And in Honolulu, when your friend the whaler asks you to take a 'fid' with him, it is simple etiquette to say, 'Here's eighteen hundred barrels, old salt!' But, 'Drink hearty!' is universal. That is the orthodox reply, the world over.

In San Francisco sometimes, if you offend a man, he proposes to take his coat off, and inquires, 'Are you on it?' If you are, you can take your coat off, too. In Virginia City, in former times, the insulted party, if he were a true man, would lay his hand gently on his six-shooter and say, 'Are you heeled?' But in Honolulu, if Smith offends Jones, Jones asks (with rising inflection on the last word, which is excessively aggravating), 'How much do you weigh?' Smith replies, 'Sixteen hundred and forty pound—and you?' 'Two ton to a dot, at a quarter past eleven this forenoon—peel yourself; you're my blubber!'

When I began this letter I meant to furnish some facts and figures concerning the great Pacific whaling traffic, to the end that San Francisco might take into consideration the expediency of making an effort to divert the patronage of the fleet to herself, if it seemed well to do so; and chiefly I meant to try and explain why that patronage does not gravitate to that center naturally and of its own accord. True, many know the reason already, and need no explanation, but many more do not understand it so well or know so much about it. But not being in a sufficiently serious mood to-day, I have wisely left for my next letter the discussion of a subject of such overwhelming gravity.*

MARK TWAIN

Reprinted from the Sacramento Weekly Union
May 26, 1866.

*The next letter, concerned chiefly with statistics, is indeed of such overwhelming gravity, that the editor, in the interest of unity, has omitted it from this volume.

THE KALIHI VALLEY

April — 1866

I HAVE ridden up the handsome Nuuanu Valley; noted the mausoleum of the departed Kings of Hawaii by the wayside; admired the neat residences, surrounded by beautiful gardens that border the turnpike; stood, at last, after six miles of travel, on the famous *Pari*—the 'divide,' we would call it—and looked down the precipice of six or eight hundred feet, over which old Kamehameha I drove the army of the King of Oahu three-quarters of a century ago; and gazed upward at the sharp peak close at my left, springing several hundred feet above my head like a colossal church spire—stood there and saw the sun go down and the little plain below and the sea that bordered it become shrouded in thick darkness; and then saw the full moon rise up and touch the tops of the billows, skip over the gloomy valley and paint the upper third of the high peak as white as silver; and heard the ladies say: 'Oh, beautiful!—and *such* a strong contrast!' and heard the gentlemen remark: 'By George! talk about scenery! how's that?'

It was all very well, but the same place in daylight does not make so fine a picture as the *Kalihi* Valley (pronounced *Kah-lee-he*, stress on the second syllable). All citizens talk about the *Pari*; all strangers visit it the first thing; all scribblers write about it—but nobody talks or writes about or visits the Pari's charming neighbor, the Kalihi Valley. I think it was a fortunate accident that led me to stumble into this enchanted ground.

For a mile or two we followed a trail that branched off from the terminus of the turnpike that leads past the Government prison, and bending close around the rocky point of a foothill we found ourselves fairly in the valley, and the panorama began to move. After a while the trail took the course of a brook that came down the center of the narrowing canyon, and followed it faithfully throughout its eccentric windings. On either side the ground rose gradually for a short distance, and then came the mountain barriers—densely wooded precipices on the right and left, that towered hundreds of feet above us, and up which one might climb about as easily as he could climb up the side of a house.

It was a novel sort of scenery, those mountain walls. Face around and look straight across at one of them, and sometimes it presented a bold, square front, with small inclination out of the perpendicular; move on a little and look back, and it was full of sharp ridges, bright with sunlight, and with deep, shady clefts between; and what had before seemed a smooth bowlder, set in among the thick shrubbery on the face of the wall, was now a bare rampart of stone that projected far out from the mass of green foliage, and was as sharply defined against the sky as if it had been built of solid masonry by the hand of man. Ahead the mountains looked portly—swollen, if you please—and were marked all over, up and down, diagonally and crosswise, by sharp ribs that reminded one of the fantastic ridges which the wind builds of the drifting snow on a plain. Sometimes these ridges were drawn all about the upper quarter of a mountain, checking it off in velvety green squares and diamonds and triangles, some beaming with sunlight and others softly shaded—the whole upper part of the mountain looking something like a vast green veil thrown over some object that had a good many edges and corners to it—then a sort of irregular 'eaves' all around, and from this the main body of the mountain swept down, with a slight outward curve, to the valley below. All over these highlands the forest trees grew so thickly that, even close at hand, they seemed like solid banks of foliage. These trees were principally of two kinds—the *koa* and the *kukui* —the one with a very light green leaf and the other with a dark green. Occasionally there were broad alternate belts of each extending diagonally from the mountain's bases to their summits and here and there, in the midst of the dark green, were great patches of the bright light-colored leaves, so that, to look far down the valley, along the undulating front of the barrier of peaks, the effect was as if the sun were streaming down upon it through breaks and rifts in the clouds, lighting up belts at intervals all along, and leaving those intervening darkened by the shadows of the clouds; and yet there was not a shred of a cloud in the whole firmament! It was very soft, and dreamy, and beautiful. And following down the two tall ridges that walled the valley in, we saw them terminate at last in two bold, black headlands that came together like a V, and across this gate ran a narrow zone of the most brilliant light green tint (the shoal water of the distant sea, between reef and shore), and beyond this the somber blue of the deeper water stretched away to the horizon. The varied picture of the lights and shadows on the wooded mountains, the strong, dark outlines of the gate, and the bright green water and the belt of blue beyond, was one replete with charming contrasts and beautiful effects—a revelation of fairyland itself.

The mountain stream beside us, brawling over its rocky bed, leaped over a miniature precipice occasionally, and then reposed for a season in a limpid pool at her base, reflecting the dank and dripping vines and ferns that clung to the wall and protruded in bunches and festoons through breaks in the sparkling cascade. On the gentle rising ground about us were shady groves of forest trees—the *ko*, the *koa*, the bread-fruit, the *lau hala*, the orange, lime, *kukui*, and many others; and, handsomest of all, the *ohia*, with its feathery tufts of splendid vermillion-tinted blossoms, a coloring so vivid as to be almost painful to the eye. Large tracts were covered with large *hau* (how) bushes, whose sheltering foliage is so thick as to be almost impervious to rain. It is spotted all over with a rich yellow flower, shaped something like a teacup, and sometimes it is further embellished by innumerable white bell-shaped blossoms, that grow upon a running vine with a name unknown to me. Here and there were wide crops of bushes completely overgrown and hidden beneath the glossy green leaves of another species of vine, and so dense was this covering that it would hardly be possible for a bird to fly through it. Then there were open spaces well carpeted with grass, and sylvan avenues that wound hither and thither till they lost themselves among the trees. In one open spot a vine of the species I last mentioned had taken possession of two tall dead stumps and wound around and about them, and swung out from their tops and twined their meeting tendrils together into a faultless arch. Man, with all his art, could not have improved its symmetry.

Verily, with its rank luxuriance of vines and blossoms, its groves of forest trees, its shady nooks and grassy lawns, its crystal brook and its wild and beautiful mountain scenery, with that charming far-off glimpse of the sea, Kalihi is the Valley of Enchantment come again!

While I am on the subject of scenery, I might as well speak of Sam Brannan's palace, or 'the Bungalow,' as it is popularly called. Years ago it was built and handsomely furnished by Shillaber, now of San Francisco, at a cost of between thirty and forty thousand dollars, and in the day of its glory must have considerably outshone its regal neighbor, the palace of the king. It was a large mansion, with compact walls of coral; dimensions, say, 60 or 70 feet front and 80 feet depth, perhaps, including the ample verandah or portico in front; this portico was supported by six or eight tall fluted Corinthian columns, some three feet in diameter; a dozen coral steps led up to the portico from the ground, and these extended the whole length of the front; there were four rooms on the main floor, some twenty-four feet square, each, and about twenty feet high, besides a room or so of smaller dimensions. When its white paint was new, this must have been a very stately edifice. But finally it passed into Brannan's hands—for the sum of thirty thousand dollars (never mind the particulars of the transaction)—and it has been going to decay for the past ten years. It has arrived there now, and it is the completest ruin I ever saw. One or two of the pillars have fallen, and lie like grand Theban ruins, diagonally across the wide portico; part of the roof of the portico has caved down, and a huge gridiron of plasterless lathing droops from above and threatens the head of the apostrophizing stranger; the windows are dirty, and some of them broken; the shutters are unhinged; the elegant doors are marred and splintered; within, the floors are strewn with *debris* from the shattered ceilings, weeds grow in damp mold in obscure corners; lizards peep curiously out from unsuspected hiding-places and then skurry along the walls and disappear in gaping crevices; the Summer breeze sighs fitfully through the desolate chambers, and the unforbidden sun looks down through many a liberal vent in roof and ceiling. The spacious grounds without are rank with weeds, and the fences are crazy with age and chronic debility. No more complete and picturesque ruin than the Bungalow exists to-day in the old world or the new. It is the most discouraged-looking pile the sun visits on its daily round, perhaps. In the sorrowful expression of its deserted halls, its fallen columns and its decayed magnificence, it seems to proclaim, in the homely phrase of California, that it has 'got enough pie.'

Thomas Jefferson John Quincy Adams, of San Francisco, agent for the State Agricultural Society of California, and agent of pretty much all the other institutions of the kind in the world, including the Paris Exhibition, who has traveled all over these islands during the past eight months, and gathered more information, and collected more silk worms, and flowers, and seeds, and done more work, and staid longer in people's houses an uninvited guest, and got more terrific hints and had a rougher time generally, on an imperceptible income, than any other man the century has produced, is Sam Brannan's trusted agent to put the Bungalow in elegant repair and draw on him for five thousand dollars for the purpose. It is not possible for me to say when the work will be commenced or who will take the daring contract—but I *can* say that so small a sum as five thousand dollars expended on the Bungalow would only spoil it as an attractive ruin, without making it amount to much as a human habitation. Let it alone, Brannan, and give your widely known and much discussed agent another job.

The King's palace stands not far from the melancholy Bungalow, in the center of grounds extensive enough to accommodate a village. The place is surrounded by neat and substantial coral walks, but the gates pertaining to them are out of repair, and so was the soldier who admitted us—or at any rate his uniform was. He was an exception, however, for the native soldiers usually keep their uniforms in good order.

The palace is a large, roomy frame building, and was very well furnished once, though now some of the appurtenances have lost some of their elegance. But the King don't care, I suppose, as he spends nearly all his time at his modest country residence at Waikiki. A large apartment in the center of the building serves as the royal council chamber; the walls are hung with life-size portraits of various European monarchs, sent hither as tokens of that cousinly regard which exists between all kings, at least on paper. To the right is the reception-room or hall of audience, and to the left are the library and a sort of ante-room or private audience chamber. In one of these are life-size portraits of old Kamehameha the Great and one or two Queens and Princes. The old war-horse had a dark brown, broad and beardless face, with native intelligence apparent in it, and something of a crafty expression about the eye; hair white with age and cropped short; in the picture he is clad in a white shirt, long red vest and with the famous feather war-cloak over all. We were permitted to examine the original cloak. It is very ample in its dimensions, and is made entirely of the small, silky, bright yellow feathers of the man-of-war or tropic bird, closely woven into a strong, coarse netting of grass by a process which promises shortly to become a lost art, inasmuch as only one native, and he an old man, is left who understands it in its highest elegance. These feathers are rare and costly, because each bird has but two of them—one under each wing—and the birds are not plenty. It required several generations to collect the materials and manufacture this cloak, and had the work been performed in the United States, under our fine army contract system it would have cost the Government more millions of dollars than

I can estimate without a large arithmetic and a blackboard. In old times, when a king put on his gorgeous feather war-cloak, it meant trouble; some other king and his subjects were going to catch it. We were shown other war-cloaks, made of yellow feathers, striped and barred with broad bands of red ones—fine specimens of barbaric splendor. The broken spear of a terrible chief who flourished seven hundred years ago, according to the tradition, was also brought out from among the sacred relics of a former age and displayed. It is said that this chieftain stood seven feet high without his boots (he was permanently without them), and was able to snake an enemy out of the ranks with this spear at a distance of forty to sixty, and even a hundred feet; and the spear, of hard, heavy, native wood, was once thirty feet long. The name of this pagan hero is sounded no more from the trumpet of fame, his bones lie none know where, and the record of his gallant deeds is lost. But he was a 'brick,' we may all depend upon that. How the wood of the weapon has managed to survive seven centuries of decay, though, is a question calculated to worry the antiquaries.

But it is sunrise, now, and time for honest people to begin to 'turn in.'

MARK TWAIN

Reprinted from the Sacramento Weekly Union
June 2, 1866.

HAWAIIAN LEGISLATURE

May 23, 1866

I HAVE been reporting the Hawaiian Legislature all day. This is my first visit to the Capitol. I expected to be present on the 25th of April and see the King open his Parliament in state and hear his speech, but I was in Maui then and Legislatures had no charms for me.

The Government of the Hawaiian Kingdom is composed of three estates, viz: The King, the Nobles and the Commons or Representatives. The Nobles are members of the Legislature by right of their nobility—by blood, if you please—and hold the position for life. They hold the right to sit, at any rate, though that right is not complete until they are formally commissioned as Legislators by the King. Prince William, who is thirty-one years of age, was only so commissioned two years ago, and is now occupying a seat in the Parliament for the first time. The King's Ministers belong to the Legislature by virtue of their office. Formerly the Legislative Assembly consisted of a House of Nobles and a House of Representatives, and worked separately, but now both estates sit and vote together. The object of the change was to strengthen the hands of the Nobles by giving them a chance to overawe the Commons (the latter being able to outvote the former by about three to one), and it works well. The handful of Nobles and Ministers, being backed by the King and acting as his mouthpieces, outweigh the common multitude on the other side of the House, and carry things pretty much their own way. It is well enough, for even if the Representatives were to assert their strength and override the Nobles and pass a law which did not suit the King, His Majesty would veto the measure and that would be the end of it, for there is no passing a bill over *his* veto.

Once, when the legislative bodies were separate and the Representatives did not act to suit the late King (Kamehameha IV), he took Cromwell's course—prorogued the Parliament instanter and sent the members about their business. When the present King called a Convention, a year or two ago, to frame a new Constitution, he wanted a property qualification to vote incorporated (universal suffrage was the rule before) and desired other amendments, which the Convention refused to sanction. He dismissed them at once, and fixed the Constitution up to suit himself, ratified it, and it is now the fundamental law of the land, although it has never been formally ratified and accepted by the people or the Legislature. He took back a good deal of power which his predecessors had surrendered to the people, abolished the universal suffrage clause and denied the privilege of voting to all save such as were possessed of a hundred dollars' worth of real estate or had an income of seventy-five dollars a year. And, if my opinion were asked, I would say he did a wise thing in this last named matter.

The King is invested with very great power. But he is a man of good sense and excellent education, and has an extended knowledge of business, which he acquired through long and arduous training as Minister of the Interior under the late King, and therefore he uses his vast authority wisely and well.

The Legislature meets in the Supreme Court-room, an apartment which is larger, lighter and better fitted and furnished than any court-room in San Francisco. A railing across the center separates the legislators from the visitors.

When I got to the main entrance of the building, and was about to march boldly in, I found myself confronted by a large placard, upon which was printed:

NO ADMITTANCE BY THIS ENTRANCE EXCEPT TO MEMBERS OF THE LEGISLATURE AND FOREIGN OFFICIALS

It shocked my republican notions somewhat, but I pocketed the insinuation that I was not high-toned enough to go in at the front door, and went around and entered meekly at the back one. If I ever come to these islands again I will come as the Duke of San Jose, and put on as many frills as the best of them.

I found the Legislature to consist of half a dozen white men and some thirty or forty natives. It was a dark assemblage. The Nobles and Ministers (about a dozen of them altogether) occupied the extreme left of the hall, with David Kalakaua (the King's Chamberlain) and Prince William at the head. The President of the Assembly, His Royal Highness M. Kekuanaoa, and the Vice President (Rhodes) sat in the pulpit, if I may so term it.

The President is the King's father. He is an erect, strongly built, massive featured, white-haired, swarthy old gentleman of 80 years of age or thereabouts. He was simply but well dressed, in a blue cloth coat and white vest, and white pantaloons, without spot, dust or blemish upon them. He bears himself with a calm, stately dignity, and is a man of noble presence. He was a young man and a distinguished warrior under that terrific old fighter, Kamehameha I, more than half a century ago, and I could not help saying to myself, 'This man, naked as the day he was born, and war-club and spear in hand, has charged at the head of a horde of savages against other hordes of savages far back in the past, and reveled in slaughter and carnage; has worshiped wooden images on his bended knees; has seen hundreds of his race offered up in heathen temples as sacrifices to hideous idols, at a time when no missionary's foot had ever pressed this soil, and he had never heard of the white man's God; has believed his enemy could secretly pray him to death; has seen the day, in his childhood, when it was a crime punishable by death for a man to eat with his wife, or for a plebeian to let his shadow fall upon the King—and now look at him: an educated Christian; neatly and handsomely dressed; a high-minded, elegant gentleman; a traveler, in some degree, and one who has been the honored guest of royalty in Europe; a man practiced in holding the reins of an enlightened government, and well versed in the politics of his country and in general, practical information. Look at him, sitting there presiding over the deliberations of a legislative body, among whom are white men—a grave, dignified, statesmanlike personage, and as seemingly natural and fitted to the place as if he had been born in it and had never been out of it in his life time. Lord! how the experiences of this old man's strange, eventful life must shame the cheap inventions of romance!'

Kekuanaoa is not of the blood royal. He derives his princely rank from his wife, who was a daughter of Kamehameha the Great. Under other monarchies the male line takes precedence of the female in tracing genealogies, but here the opposite is the case—the female line takes precedence. Their reason for this is exceedingly sensible, and I recommend it to the aristocracy of Europe: They say it is easy to know who a man's mother was, but, etc., etc.

The mental caliber of the Legislative Assembly is up to the average of such bodies the world over—and I wish it were a compliment to say it, but it is hardly so. I have seen a number of Legislatures, and there was a comfortable majority in each of them that knew just about enough to come in when it rained, and that was all. Few men of first class ability can afford to let their affairs go to ruin while they fool away their time in Legislatures for months on a stretch. Few such men care a straw for the small-beer distinction one is able to achieve in such a place. But your chattering, one-horse village lawyer likes it, and your solemn ass from the cow counties, who don't know the Constitution from the Lord's Prayer, enjoys it, and these you will always find in the Assembly; the one gabble, gabble, gabbling threadbare platitudes and 'give-me-liberty-or-give-me-death' buncombe from morning till night, and the other asleep, with his slab-soled brogans set up like a couple of grave-stones on the top of his desk.

Among the Commons in this Legislature are a number of Kanakas, with shrewd, intelligent faces, and a 'gift of gab' that is appalling. The Nobles are able, educated, fine-looking men, who do not talk often, but when they do they generally say something—a remark which will not apply to all their white associates in the same house. If I were not ashamed to digress so often I would like to expatiate a little upon the noticeable fact that the nobility of this land, as a general thing, are distinguishable from the common herd by their large stature and commanding presence, and also set forth the theories in vogue for accounting for it, but for the present I will pass the subject by.

At 11 A. M. His Royal Highness the President called the House to order. The roll-call was dispensed with for some reason or other, and the Chaplain, a venerable looking white man, offered up a prayer in the native tongue; and I must say that this curious language, with its numerous vowels and its entire absence of hissing sounds, fell very softly and musically from his lips. A white Chief Clerk read the Journal of the preceding day's proceedings in English, and then handed the document to Bill Ragsdale, a 'half-white' (half white and half Kanaka), who translated and clattered it off in Kanaka with a volubility that was calculated to make a slow-spoken man like me distressingly nervous.

Bill Ragsdale stands up in front of the Speaker's pulpit, with his back against it, and fastens his quick black eye upon any member who rises, lets him say half a dozen sentences and then interrupts him, and repeats his speech in a loud, rapid voice, turning every Kanaka speech into English and every English speech into Kanaka, with a readiness and felicity of language that are remarkable—waits for another installment of talk from the member's lips and goes on with his translation as before. His tongue is in constant motion from eleven in the forenoon till four in the afternoon, and why it does not wear out is the affair of Providence, not mine. There is a spice of deviltry in the fellow's nature, and it crops out every now and then when he is translating the speeches of slow old Kanakas who do not understand English. Without departing from the spirit of a member's remarks, he will, with apparent unconsciousness, drop in a little voluntary contribution occasionally in the way of a word or two that will make the gravest speech utterly ridiculous. He is careful not to venture upon such experiments, though, with the remarks of persons able to detect him. I noticed when he translated for His Excellency David Kalakaua, who is an accomplished English scholar, he asked, 'Did I translate you correctly, your Excellency?' or something to that effect. The rascal.

This Legislature is like all other Legislatures. A wooden-head gets up and proposes an utterly absurd something or other, and he and half a dozen other wooden-heads discuss it with windy vehemence for an hour, the remainder of the house sitting in silent patience the while, and then a sensible man—a man of weight—a big gun—gets up and shows the foolishness of the matter in five sentences; a vote is taken and the thing is tabled. Now, on one occasion, a Kanaka member, who paddled over here from some barren rock or other out yonder in the ocean—some scaliwag who wears nothing but a pair of socks and a plug hat when he is at home, or possibly is even more scantily arrayed in the popular *malo*—got up and gravely gave notice of a bill to authorize the construction of a suspension bridge from Oahu to Hawaii, a matter of a hundred and fifty miles! He said the natives would prefer it to the inter-island schooners, and they wouldn't suffer from sea-sickness on it. Up came Honorables Ku and Kulaui, and Kowkow and Kiawawhoo and a lot of other clacking geese, and harried and worried this notable internal improvement until some sensible person rose and choked them off by moving the previous question. Do not do an unjust thing now, and imagine Kanaka Legislatures do stupider things than other similar bodies. Rather blush to remember that once, when a Wisconsin Legislature had the affixing of a penalty for the crime of arson under consideration, a member got up and seriously suggested that when a man committed the damning crime of arson they ought either to hang him or make him marry the girl! To my mind the suspension bridge man was a Solomon compared to this idiot.

(I shall have to stop at this point and finish this subject to-morrow. There is a villain over the way, yonder, who has been playing 'Get out of the Wilderness' on a flute ever since I sat down here to-night, sometimes fast, sometimes slow, and always skipping the first note in the second bar—skipping it so uniformly that I have got to waiting and painfully looking out for it latterly. Human nature cannot stand this sort of torture. I wish his funeral was to come off at half-past eleven o'clock to-morrow and I had nothing to do. I would attend it.)

It has been six weeks since I touched a pen. In explanation and excuse I offer the fact that I spent that time (with the exception of one week) on the island of Maui. I only got back yesterday. I never spent so pleasant a month before, or bade any place good-bye so regretfully. I doubt if there is a mean person there, from the homeliest man on the island (Lewers) down to the oldest (Tallant). I went to Maui to stay a week and remained five. I had a jolly time. I would not have fooled away any of it writing letters under any consideration whatever. It will be five or six weeks before I write again. I sail for the island of Hawaii to-morrow, and my Maui notes will not be written up until I come back.

MARK TWAIN

Reprinted from the Sacramento Weekly Union
June 23, 1866.

THE SOLONS AT WORK

May 23, 1866.

THE first business that was transacted to-day was the introduction of a bill to prohibit the intermarrying of old persons with young ones, because of the non-fruitfulness of such unions. The measure was discussed, laughed over, and finally tabled. I will remark here that I noticed that there seemed to be no regular order of business observed. Motions, resolutions, notices, introduction and third reading of bills, etc., were jumbled together. This may be convenient enough for the members, but it must necessarily be troublesome to the clerks and reporters.

Then a special Committee reported back favorably a bill to prohibit Chinamen from removing their male children from the islands, and the report was adopted—which I thought was rather hard on the Chinamen.

Next 'the gentleman from Kohala' offered a resolution requesting the Minister of the Interior to bring his books into the House and separate the 'Bishop of England's' printing account from his omnibus of 'sundries,' and show just how my Lord's account with the Government printing office stood. [Sensation.]

A member jumped up and moved to amend by requesting a general inquisition into printing affairs, and to strike out the offensive clause particularizing the Bishop's bill.

The Minister of the Interior (an Englishman—Dr. Hutchinson) opposed the motion, angrily—said it 'showed the animus of the thing the way it stood.' He said he was ready to produce the books, and went at once and brought them in.

Another member moved to table the original motion.

Harris, Minister of Finance, wanted the motion to stand unamended; he said it showed the animus of the thing, too; said it was the old insinuation, emanating from outside the walls of this House—that the Minister of the Interior was diverting the public funds to the support of the Anglican church; the ancient insinuation that he was recreant to his duty, etc.; said the animus was prominent enough in the language of the resolution, which denied to the Lord Bishop of Honolulu the title which all the world recognized as his, and called him the 'Bishop of England;' said the Bishop always paid his bills; he (Harris) always paid his bills, and gave money frequently to the Anglican church; was a member of it; would like to know of a single solitary instance where the Congregationalist member from Kohala had ever contributed one dollar, one shilling, one infinitesimal fraction of a farthing to the support of the Reformed Catholic Church of the Lord Bishop; but a King's Minister couldn't be honest, oh no! and a Minister couldn't be a gentleman—certainly not! impossible!—oh, utterly!

And so forth and so on, wandering further and further from the question before the House, and quacking about stuff that had no more to do with the subject under discussion than the Decalogue has got to do with the Declaration of Independence. This man was on his feet every five minutes for an hour. One timid Commoner feebly moved the previous question once, with a vague hope of shutting up the Minister, but he never got a second, and was snubbed in a moment, and 'went in his hole,' as they say in California.

The original motion was finally tabled, but it made a fearful stir among the Ministers during its brief existence. It created a bitter discussion, and showed how malignant are the jealousies that rankle in the breasts of rival religious denominations here.

The Vice President said he was sorry the motion had been offered; that it was an insult to the Government, to the Bishop of Honolulu, to the House, and to all parties concerned, and it grieved him to have to put it to a vote.

In the debate, His Excellency Minister Harris was the champion of the Reformed Catholic Church (though, to save my soul, I could not see what *any* Church had to do—that is, openly and aboveboard—with the question before the House). He was the champion; and without any ill feeling toward him I will yet express the conviction that about two more such champions would bring ruin and destruction upon any cause under the sun.

Minister Harris is six feet high, bony and rather slender, middle-aged; has long, ungainly arms; stands so straight that he leans back a little; has small side whiskers; from my distance his eyes seemed blue, and his teeth looked too regular and too white for an honest man; he has a long head the wrong way—that is, up and down; and a bogus Roman nose and a great, long, cadaverous undertaker's countenance, displayed upon which his ghastly attempts at humorous expressions were as shocking as a facetious leer on the face of a corpse. He is a native of New Hampshire, but is unworthy of the name of American. I think, from his manner and language to-day, that he belongs, body and soul, and boots, to the King of the Sandwich Islands and the 'Lord Bishop of Honolulu.'

He has no command of language—or ideas. His oratory is all show and pretense; he makes considerable noise and a great to do, and impresses his profoundest incoherencies with an oppressive solemnity and ponderous windmill gesticulations with his flails. He raises his hand aloft and looks piercingly at the interpreter and launches out into a sort of prodigious declamation, thunders upward higher and higher toward his climax—words, words, awful four-syllable words, given with convincing emphasis that almost inspires them with meaning, and just as you take a sustaining breath and 'stand by' for the crash, his poor little rocket fizzes faintly in the zenith and goes out ignominiously. The sensation one experiences is the same a miner feels when he puts in a blast which he thinks will send the whole top of a mountain to the moon, and after running a quarter of a mile in ten seconds to get out of the way, is disgusted to hear it make a trifling, dull report, discharge a pipe-full of smoke, and barely jolt half a bushel of dirt. After one of these incomprehensible ravings, Mr. Harris bends bown and smiles a horrid smile of self-complacency in the face of the Minister of the Interior; bends to the other side and continues it in the face of the Minister of Foreign Affairs; beams it serenely upon the admiring lobby, and finally confers the remnants of it upon the unhappy interpreter—all of which pantomime says as plainly as words could say it: 'Eh?—but wasn't it an awful shot?' Harris says the weakest and most insipid things, and then tries by the expression of his countenance to swindle you into the conviction that they are the most blighting sarcasms. And in seven years I have never lost my cheerfulness and wanted to lay me down in some secluded spot and die, and be at rest, until I heard him try to be funny to-day. If I had had a double-barrelled shotgun I would have blown him into a million fragments. Harris deals in long paragraphs of personalities, that would not be permitted in any other Legislature. This man has the reputation of being an 'able' man; yet he was talking pretty much all the time to-day, and all the good sound sense or point there was in his vaporings could have been boiled down into half a page of foolscap. Harris is *not* a man of first-class abilities—but that is only my opinion, you know—not Harris'. He knows some things, though. He knows that his salary of $4,000 is little enough, in all conscience (especially as he gets nothing as Acting Attorney General, and is not allowed to engage in outside business), and he knew enough on one occasion to vote against reducing his pay to $3,000 when his single vote was necessary to kill the proposed economy. He is an inveterate official barnacle, and is generally well supplied with offices—some people say the Hawaiian Government is a wheelbarrow, and that Harris is the wheel.

The Legislature voted an appropriation yesterday to have the photographs of its members taken and hung up in the Capitol. If they had known I was going to paint Harris, they might have saved about three dollars. Harris, you won't do.

If I had time now I would write you a little something about Harris. Under the circumstances, though, I feel it my duty to pass on to something else.

Next to His Excellency Mr. Harris, His Majesty's Minister of Finance, sits His Excellency Mr. Hutchinson, His Majesty's Minister of the Interior—an Englishman. He has sandy hair, sandy mustache, sandy complexion—is altogether one of the sandiest men I ever saw, so to speak; is a tall, stoop-shouldered, middle-aged, lowering-browed, intense-eyed, irascible man, and looks like he might have his little prejudices and partialities. He has got one good point, however—he don't talk.

Near Dr. Hutchinson sit His Excellency the Governor of Oahu (born in this country of Italian and American parentage, and considered an American) and His Excellency M. De Varigny, Acting Minister of Foreign Affairs—a Frenchman. These are merely sensible, unpretentious men—nothing particularly remarkable about their manner or appearance. If Varigny were as hopelessly bad as his English pronunciation, nothing but a special intervention of Providence could save him from perdition hereafter.

I have found at least one startling peculiarity about this Hawaiian Legislature. They do not accuse its members of being stained with bribery and corruption. It is a new and pleasant sensation to me. Some people ascribe this singular purity to innate virtue, while others less charitable say the members are not offered bribes because they are such leaky vessels that they would be sure to let it out. Doubtless, in some cases one theory is correct, and the other correct in other cases. I hope it is somehow that way; at any rate, I haven't time to discuss it.

Legislative etiquette is of a low grade everywhere, I believe. I find no exception to the rule here. All hands smoke during the session, from the highest down to the pock-marked messenger. Cow county members—or perhaps I should say taro-patch members—lay the sides of their faces on the desks, encircle them with their arms and go to sleep for a few moments at a time. I know they must put their feet on the desks sometimes, but I could not catch them at it. I saw them eating crackers and cheese, though, and freely excused them for it, because they hold long, fatiguing sessions—from eleven till four o'clock, without intermission. I am grieved to say that their etiquette is a shade superior to that of the early Washoe Legislature. 'Horse Williams' was a member of one of them, and he used to always prop his vast feet upon his desk and get behind them and eat a raw turnip during prayer by the Chaplain.

So much for the Legislature. I came away and left them at

the favorite occupation of such bodies—crowding the finance officer's estimates to the utmost limit. The last thing they did was to provide a Clerk for the Sheriff of Maui, with a salary of $1,000, which was well enough, considering that for $2,000 a year and some trifling perquisites, that officer acts as Sheriff of the Island of Maui, Postmaster of Lahaina, Custom-house officer, Tax Collector of the Island of Lauai, and probably does a little in a general way in the missionary line, though he is better at entertaining a temporary guest, as I am aware; but you know the inevitable result—every Sheriff of every little dab of rock in this group will have to have a thousand-dollar clerk now.

Brown has been keeping a sharp lookout for the King for nearly three months, now. When we came out of the Capitol we heard His Majesty had been at the door a few minutes before. Said the impetuous child of nature:

'Blame that King, ain't I ever—'

'Peace, son!' said I; 'respect the sacred name of royalty.'

Speaking of the King reminds me of something which ought to be said and might as well be said in this paragraph. Some people in California have an idea that the King of the Sandwich Islands is a man who spends his time idling about the town of Honolulu with individuals of questionable respectability, and drinking habitually and to excess. This impression is wrong. Before he ascended the throne he was 'faster' than was well for him or for his good name, but, like the hero of Agincourt, he renounced his bad habits and discarded his Falstaffs when he became King, and since that time has conducted himself as becomes his high position. He attends closely to his business, makes no display, does not go about much, and in manners and habits is a thorough gentleman. He only appears in the streets when his affairs require it, and then he goes well mounted or in his carriage, and decently and properly attended.

And while upon this subject I will remark that His Majesty's income is amply sufficient for the modest state he indulges in. The Legislature appropriates $16,000 a year to his use, and his estates (called the 'Royal Domain'), yield him $20,000 a year besides. The present palace is to be pulled down and a new one erected. The Legislature has just made an appropriation of $40,000 to begin the work and carry it on for the next two years. There was nothing said about what it is ultimately to cost—wherefore I surmise that it is the design of the Government to build a palace well worthy of the name.

MARK TWAIN

Reprinted from the Sacramento Weekly Union
June 23, 1866.

DEATH OF A PRINCESS

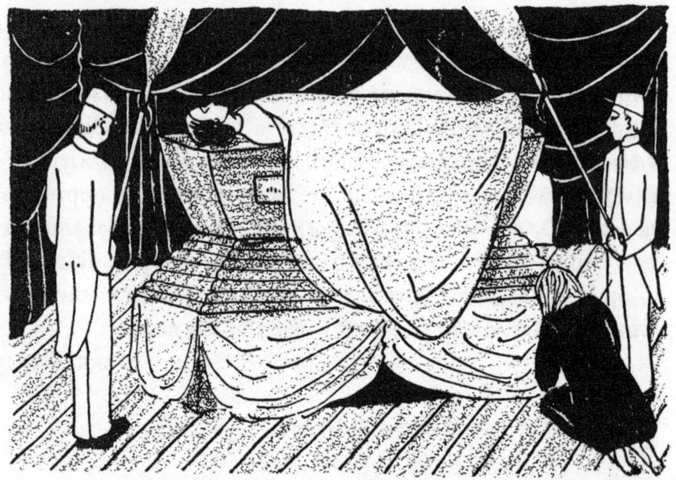

June 22, 1866

I HAVE just got back from a three weeks' cruise on the island of Hawaii and an eventful sojourn of several days at the great volcano. But of that trip I will speak hereafter. I am too badly used up to do it now. I only want to write a few lines at present by the Live Yankee, merely to keep my communications open, as the soldiers say.

I find Hawaiian politics in a state of unusual stir on account of the death of the King's sister, Her Royal Highness the Princess Victoria Kamamalu Kaahumanu, heir presumptive to the crown. She was something over twenty-seven years old, and had never been married, although she was formally betrothed to Prince William and the marriage day appointed more than once, but circumstances interfered and the nuptials were never consummated.

The Princess was a granddaughter of old Kamehameha the Conqueror, and like all of that stock, was talented. She was the last female descendant of the old warrior.

The care of her infancy was confided to Dr. A. F. Judd (afterward so honorably distinguished in Hawaiian history). Subsequently Hon. John Ii was appointed her guardian by the King. She was carefully educated in the Royal Chief School, which was at that time presided over by the earliest friends of the Hawaiians, the American Missionaries. (It is now in the hands of the gentlemen of the Royal Hawaiian Church, otherwise the 'Reformed Catholic Church,' a sort of nondescript wildcat religion imported here from England.) She became an accomplished pianist and vocalist, and for many years sat at the melodeon and led the choir in the great stone church here. From her infancy it was expected that she would one day fill the throne, and therefore great importance was attached to her acts, and they were duly observed and noted as straws calculated to show how the wind would be likely to set in her ultimate official life. Consequently the strong friendship she manifested for the missionaries was regarded with jealous eye in certain quarters, and frequent attempts were made to diminish her partiality for them. The late Mr. Wyllie, Minister of Foreign Affairs (a native of Scotland), once sent for Hon. Mr. Ii, and endeavored to get him to use his influence in dissuading the Princess and Mrs. Bishop (a high chiefess who visited California in the *Ajax* lately), from further attendance upon the church choirs. He said it was very improper and out of character for princesses to sing in a choir, and that such personages in England would not do such a thing. The effort was fruitless, however; Victoria continued her former course, and remained faithful to her early friends. She was urged to desert them and go over to the Reformed Catholic Church, but she steadfastly refused.

The Princess was distinguished as the founder and Perpetual President of a benevolent association called 'Aha Hui Kaahumanu'—an organization partaking of the benevolent character of Freemasonry, but without its secrecy. It was composed of her countrywomen, and supported by their subscriptions; its membership was exceedingly numerous, and its ramifications extended all over the several islands of the group. Its objects were to secure careful nursing of its members when sick, and their decent burial after death. The society always formed in procession and followed deceased members to the grave, arrayed in a uniform composed of a white robe and a scarf, which indicated the official rank of the wearer by its color.

The Princess was possessed of immense landed estates, and formerly kept up considerable state. She rode in a fine carriage, and had her guards and sentries about her several residences, in European fashion.

The natives have always been remarkable for the extravagant love and devotion they show toward their chiefs; it almost amounts to worship. When Victoria was a girl of fifteen she made an excursion through the island of Hawaii (the realm of the ancient founders of her race), with her guardian and a retinue of servants, and was everywhere received with a wild enthusiasm by her people. In Hilo, they came in multitudes to the house of the reverend missionary, where she was stopping, and brought with them all manner of offerings—poi, taro, bananas, pigs, fowls—anything they got hold of which was valuable in their eyes—and many of them stinted and starved themselves for the time being, no doubt, to do this honor to a Princess who could not use or carry away the hundredth part of what they lavished upon her. And for hours and even days together the people thronged around the place and wept and chanted their distressing songs, and wailed their agonizing wails; for joy at the return of a loved one and sorrow at his death are expressed in precisely the same way with this curious people.

The Princess died on Tuesday, May 29th, and on Wednesday the body was conveyed to the King's palace, there to lie in state about four weeks, which is royal custom here. The chamber is still darkened, and its walls and ceilings draped and festooned with solemn black. The corpse is attired in white satin, trimmed with lace and ruche, and reposes upon the famous yellow-feather war-cloak of the Kings of Hawaii; a simple coronet of orange blossoms, interwoven with white feathers, adorns the head that was promised a regal diadem; six *kahili*-bearers stand upon each side, and these are surrounded by a guard of honor in command of one of the High Chiefs; a party of Chief women are in constant attendance, and officers of the household troops and of the volunteer forces are on duty about the palace; the old Queen Dowager sleeps in the chamber every night. Candelabras burn day and night at the head and feet of the corpse, and shed a funereal twilight over it, and over the silent attendants and the dark and dismal symbols of woe. Every evening a new chant, composed by some Chief woman several days before, and carefully rehearsed, is sung. All this in the death chamber.

Outside, on the broad verandahs and in the ample palace yard, a multitude of common natives howl and wail, and weep and chant the dreary funeral songs of ancient Hawaii, and dance the strange dance for the dead. Numbers of these people remain there day after day and night after night, sleeping in the open air in the intervals of their mourning ceremonies.

I am told these things. I have not seen them. The King has ordered that no foreigner shall be permitted to enter the palace gates before the last night previous to the funeral. The reason why this order was issued is, I am told, that the performances at the palace at the time the corpse of the late King lay there in state were criticized and commented upon too freely. These performances were considerably toned down while the missionaries were in power, but under the more liberal regime of the new

Reformed Catholic dispensation they fell back toward their old-time barbarous character. The gates were thrown open and everybody went in and saw and heard what may be termed the funeral orgies of the dead King. The term is coarse, but perhaps it is a better one than a milder one would be. And then scribblers like myself wrote column after column about the matter in the public prints, and the subject was discussed and criticized in private circles and inveighed against in the pulpits. All this was harassing and disagreeable to the parties nearest concerned, and hence the present order forbidding any but Hawaiian citizens and lenient friends from witnessing the ceremonies. So strong is some people's curiosity, however, that the law has already been violated several times within the past week by strangers, who entered the tabooed grounds in disguise. They were discovered, however, and quietly turned out.

The deceased Princess has lain in state now for more than three weeks—yet still the nightly wailing goes on in the palace yard, and the crowds of natives who conduct it increase steadily by influx from the other islands, and the lamentations grow more extravagant all the time. The missionary efforts to discourage and break up this weird custom, inherited from the old pagan days, are quietly rebuked in a little advertisement which appears over the signature of the King's Chamberlain in the public papers to-day, wherein he invites all natives to come to the palace grounds and stay there night and day and take part in the wailing for the departed. That looks like a disposition on the part of the authorities not only to check the progress of civilization, but to go backward a little.

The Legislature have appropriated $6,000 to defray the funeral expenses of the Princess. The obsequies will take place the latter part of next week. I have seen the coffin (it is not quite finished yet), and certainly it is the most elegant piece of burial furniture I ever saw. It is made of those two superb species of native wood, ko and koa. The former is nearly as dark as ebony; the latter is like fine California laurel, richly grained and clouded with mahogany. Both woods have an iron-like hardness, and are exceedingly close in grain, and when highly polished and varnished nothing in the shape of wood can be more brilliant, more lustrous, more beautiful. It produces a sort of ecstasy in me to look at it, and holds me like a mesmeric fascination. There is nothing extraordinary about the fashioning—the planning and constructing—of this coffin, but still it is beautiful. The wood is so splendidly burnished, and so gracefully grained and clouded.

The silver tablet upon the coffin, upon which is to be inscribed the name and title of the deceased, is to cost $500. I go into these minor details to show you that royal state in the Sandwich Islands approaches as near to its European models as the circumstances of the case will admit.

If a Sandwich Islands missionary comes across a stranger, I think he weighs him and measures him and judges him (in defiance of the injunction to 'judge not,' etc.) by an ideal which he has created in his own mind—and if that stranger falls short of that ideal in any particular, the good missionary thinks he falls just that much short of what he ought to be in order to stand a chance for salvation; and with a tranquil simplicity of self-conceit, which is marvelous to a modest man, he honestly believes that the Almighty, of a necessity, thinks exactly as he does. I violate the injunction to judge not, also. I judge the missionary, but, with a modesty which is entitled to some credit, I freely confess that my judgment may err. Now, therefore, when I say that the Sandwich Islands missionaries are pious; hard-working; hard-praying; self-sacrificing; hospitable; devoted to the well-being of this people and the interests of Protestantism; bigoted; puritanical; slow; ignorant of all white human nature and natural ways of men, except the remnants of these things that are left in their own class or profession; old fogy—fifty years behind the age; uncharitable toward the weaknesses of the flesh; considering all shortcomings, faults and failings in the light of crimes, and having no mercy and no forgiveness for such—when I say this about the missionaries, I do it with the explicit understanding that it is only *my* estimate of them—not that of a Higher Intelligence—not that of even other sinners like myself. It is only *my* estimate, and it may fall far short of being a just one.

Now, after the above free confession of my creed, I think I ought to be allowed to print a word of defense of these missionaries without having that eternal charge of 'partiality and prejudice' launched at me that is generally sure to be discharged at any man here who ventures—in certain quarters—to give them any credit or offer to defend them from ill-natured aspersions.

Mr. Staley, my Lord Bishop of Honolulu—who was built into a Lord by the English Bishop of Oxford and shipped over here with a fully equipped 'Established Church' in his pocket—has frequently said that the natives of these islands are morally and religiously in a worse condition to-day than they were before the American missionaries ever came here. Now that is not true—and in that respect the statement bears a very strong family likeness to many other of the Bishop's remarks about our missionaries. Our missionaries are our missionaries—and even if they were our devils I would not want any English prelate to slander them. I will not go into an argument to prove that the natives have been improved by missionary labor—because facts are stronger than argument. Above I have stated how the natives are now singing and wailing every night—queerly enough, but innocently and harmlessly—out yonder in the palace yard, for the dead Princess. Following is some account of the style of conducting this sort of thing shortly before the traduced missionaries came. I quote from Jarves' *History of the Sandwich Islands:*

'The ceremonies observed on the death of any important personage were exceedingly barbarous. The hair was shaved or cut close, teeth knocked out and sometimes the ears were mangled. Some tattooed their tongues in a corresponding manner to the other parts of their bodies. Frequently the flesh was cut or burnt, eyes scooped out, and other even more painful personal outrages inflicted. But these usages, however shocking they may appear, were innocent compared with the horrid saturnalia which immediately followed the death of a chief of the highest rank. Then the most unbounded license prevailed; law and restraint were cast aside, and the whole people appeared more like demons than human beings. Every vice and crime was allowed. Property was destroyed, houses fired and old feuds revived and avenged. Gambling, theft and murder were as open as the day; clothing was cast aside as a useless incumbrance; drunkenness and promiscuous prostitution prevailed throughout the land, no women, excepting the widows of the deceased, being exempt from the grossest violation. There was no passion however lewd, or desire however wicked, but could be gratified with impunity during the continuance of this period, which, happily, from its own violence soon spent itself. No other nation was ever witness to a custom which so entirely threw off all moral and legal restraints and incited the evil passions to unresisted riot and wanton debauchery.'

It is easy to see, now, that the missionaries have made a better people of this race than they formerly were; and I am satisfied that if that oldtime national spree were still a custom of the country, my Lord Bishop would not be in this town to-day saying hard things about the missionaries. No; his excellent judgment would have impelled him to take to the woods when the Princess died.

The great bulk of the wealth, the commerce, the enterprise and the spirit of progress in the Sandwich Islands centers in the Americans. Americans own the whaling fleet; they own the great sugar plantations; they own the cattle ranches; they own their share of the mercantile depots and the lines of packet ships. Whatever of commercial and agricultural greatness the country can boast of it owes to them. Consequently the question of who is likely to succeed to the crown in case of the death of the present King, is an interesting one to American residents, and therefore to their countrymen at home. The incumbent of the throne has it in his power to help or hinder them a good deal. The King is not married; and if he dies without leaving an heir of his own body or appointing a successor, the crown will be likely to fall upon either His Highness Prince William C. Lunalilo or David Kalakaua. The former is of the highest blood in the kingdom—higher than the King himself, it is said—and Kalakaua is descended from the ancient Kings of the island of Hawaii. King Keoua (father of Kamehameha the Great), great-great-grandfather of the present King, was also the great-great-grandfather of Prince William; but from Kamehameha the lines diverge, and if there is any kinship between William and Kamehameha V, it is distant. They both had a common ancestor in King Umi, however, a gentleman who flourished several hundred years ago. Prince William is called eleventh in descent from Umi, and the present King only fourteenth, which confers seniority of birth and rank upon the former. But this subject is tanglesome.

Prince William is a man of fine, large build; is thirty-one years of age; is affable, gentlemanly, open, frank, manly; is as independent as a lord and has a spirit and a will like the old Conqueror himself. He is intelligent, shrewd, sensible—is a man of first rate abilities, in fact. He has a right handsome face, and the best nose in the Hawaiian kingdom, white or otherwise; it is a splendid beak, and worth being proud of. He has one most unfortunate fault—he drinks constantly; and it is a great pity, for if he would moderate this appetite, or break it off altogether, he would become a credit to himself and his nation. I like this man, and I like his bold independence, and his friendship for and appreciation of the American residents; and I take no pleasure in mentioning this failing of his. If I could print a sermon that would reform him, I would cheerfully do it.

Hon. David Kalakaua, who at present holds the office of King's Chamberlain, is a man of fine presence, is an educated gentleman and a man of good abilities. He is approaching forty, I should judge—is thirty-five, at any rate. He is conservative, politic and calculating, makes little display, and does not talk much in the Legislature. He is a quiet, dignified, sensible man, and would do no discredit to the kingly office.

The King has power to appoint his successor. If he does such a thing, his choice will probably fall on Kalakaua. In case the King should die without making provision for a successor, it would be the duty of the Legislature to select a king from among the dozen high Chiefs, male and female, who are eligible under the Hawaiian Constitution. Under these circumstances, if Prince William were thoroughly redeemed from his besetting sin, his chances would be about even with Kalakaua's.

It is two o'clock in the morning, and I have just been up toward the palace to hear some of the singing of the numerous well-born watchers (of both sexes) who are standing guard in the chamber of death. The voices were very pure and rich, and blended together without harshness or discord, and the music was exceedingly plaintive and beautiful. I would have been glad enough to get closer. When the plebeians outside the building resumed their distressing noise I came away. In the distance I hear them at it yet, poor, simple, loving, faithful, Christian savages.

The *Swallow* arrived here on Monday morning, with Anson Burlingame, United States Minister to China, and General Van Valkenburgh, United States Minister to Japan. Their stay is limited to fourteen days, but a strong effort will be made to persuade them to break that limit and pass the Fourth of July here. They are paying and receiving visits constantly, of course, and are cordially welcomed. Burlingame is a man who would be esteemed, respected and popular anywhere, no matter whether he were among Christians or cannibals.

The people are expecting McCook, our new minister to these islands, every day.

Whartenby and Mackie, of Nevada (Cal.) arrived here in the last vessel, and will start back in a week or two. They came merely for recreation.

Several San Franciscans have come to Honolulu to locate permanently. Among them Dr. A. C. Buffum; he has a fair and growing practice. Judge Jones is another; he has already more law practice on his hands than he can well attend to. And lastly, J. J. Ayres, late one of the proprietors of the *Morning Call*, has arrived, with material for starting a newspaper and job office. He has not made up his mind yet, however, to try the experiment of a newspaper here. Sanford, late Chief Engineer of the *Ajax*, came in the last vessel, and proposes to settle in the islands—perhaps in the sugar line. He has gone to Maui to see what the chances are in that deservedly famous sugar-producing region.

A letter arrived here yesterday morning giving a meager account of the arrival on the island of Hawaii of nineteen poor starving wretches, who had been buffeting a stormy sea in an open boat for forty-three days! Their ship, the *Hornet*, from New York, with a quantity of kerosene on board, had taken fire and burned in lat. 2° north and lon. 135° west. Think of their sufferings for forty-three days and nights, exposed to the scorching heat of the center of the torrid zone, and at the mercy of a ceaseless storm! When they had been entirely out of provisions for a day or two and the cravings of hunger became insupportable, they yielded to the shipwrecked mariner's final and fearful alternative, and solemnly drew lots to determine who of their number should die to furnish food for his comrades—and then the morning mists lifted and they saw land. They are being cared for at Sanpohoihoi, a little seaside station I spent a night at two weeks ago. This boat-load was in charge of the Captain of the *Hornet*. He reports that the remainder of the persons in his ship (twenty in number) left her in two boats, under command of the first and second mates, and the three boats kept company until the night of the nineteenth day, when they got separated. No further particulars have arrived here yet, and no confirmation of the above sad story.

The American citizens of Honolulu, anxious to show to their distinguished visitors the honor and respect due them, have invited them to partake of a dinner upon some occasion before their departure. Burlingame and General Van Valkenburgh have accepted the invitation and will inform the Committee this evening what day will best suit their convenience.

MARK TWAIN

Reprinted from the Sacramento Weekly Union
July 21, 1866.

A MONTH OF MOURNING

June 30, 1866.

FOR a little more than a month, the late Princess—Her Royal Highness Victoria Kamamalu Kaahumanu, heir presumptive to the crown and sister to the King—lay in state at Iolaui Palace, the royal residence. For a little over a month, troops of natives of both sexes, drawn here from the several islands by the great event, have thronged past my door every evening on their way to the palace. Every night, and all night long, for more than thirty days, multitudes of these strange mourners have burned their candle-nut torches in the royal inclosure, and sung their funeral dirges, and danced their hula hulas, and wailed their harrowing wail for the dead. All this time we strangers have been consuming with curiosity to look within those walls and see the pagan deviltry that was going on there. But the thing was *tabu* (forbidden—we get our word 'taboo' from the Hawaiian language) to foreigners—*haoles*. The grounds were thrown open to everybody the first night, but several rowdy white people acted so unbecomingly—so shamefully, in fact—

that the King placed a strict *tabu* upon their future admittance. I was absent—on the island of Hawaii—at that time, and so I lost that one single opportunity to gratify my curiosity in this matter.

Last night was to behold the grand finale, inasmuch as the obsequies were to transpire to-day, and therefore I was a good deal gratified to learn that a few foreigners would be allowed to enter a side gate and view the performances in the palace yard from the verandah of Dr. Hutchinson's house (Minister of the Interior). I got there at a little after 8 P. M.

The verandah we occupied overlooked the royal grounds, and afforded an excellent view of the two thousand or twenty-five hundred natives sitting, densely packed together, in the glare of the torches, between our position and the palace, a hundred feet in front of us. It was a wild scene—those long rows of eager, dusky faces, with the light upon them; the band of hula girls in the center, showily attired in white bodices and pink skirts, and with wreaths of pink and white flowers and garlands of green leaves about their heads; and the strongly illuminated torch-bearers scattered far and near at intervals through the large assemblage and standing up conspicuously above the masses of sitting forms. Light enough found its way to the broad verandahs of the palace to enable us to see whatever transpired upon them with considerable distinctness. We could see nothing there, however, except two or three native sentries in red uniforms, with gleaming muskets in their hands.

Presently someone said:

'Oh, there's the King!'

'Where?'

'There—on the verandah—now, he's just passing that —. No; it's that blasted Harris.'

That is not really his Christian name, but he is usually called by that or a stronger one. I state this by way of explanation. Harris is the Minister of Finance and Attorney-General, and I don't know how many other things. He has three marked points: He is not a second Solomon; he is as vain as a peacock; he is as 'cheeky' as——however, there is no simile for *his* 'cheek.' In the Legislature, the other day, the Speaker was trying to seat a refractory member; the member knew he was strictly in order, though, and that his only crime was his opposition to the Ministry, and so he refused to sit down. Harris whispered to the interpreter: 'Tell the Speaker to let *me* have the chair a moment.' The Speaker vacated his place; Harris stepped into it, rapped fiercely with the gavel, scowled imperiously upon the intrepid commoner and ordered him to sit down. The man declined to do it. Harris commanded the Sergeant-at-Arms to seat him. After a trial, that officer said the bold representative of the people refused to permit him to seat him. Harris ordered the Sergeant to take the man out of the house—remove him by force! [Sensation—tempest, I should rather say.] The poor humbled and brow-beaten country members threw off their fears for the moment and became men; and from every part of the house they shouted: 'Come out of that chair! leave that place! put him out! put out the——!' [I have forgotten the Hawaiian phrase, but it is equivalent to 'miserable dog.'] And this terrible man, who was going to perform such wonders, vacated the Speaker's chair and went meekly back to his own place, leaving the stout opponent of the Ministry master of the field. The Legislature adjourned at once, and the excited and triumphant Kanakas burst forth into a stirring battle-hymn of the old days of Kamehameha the Great. Harris was an American once (he was born in Portsmouth, N. H.), but he is no longer one. He is *hoopilimeai* to the King. How do you like that, Mr. H.? How do you like being attacked in your own native tongue?

[NOTE TO THE READER: That long native word means—well, it means Uriah Heep boiled down—it means the soul and spirit of obsequiousness. No genuine American can be other than obedient and respectful toward the Government he lives under and the flag that protects him, but no such an American can ever be *hoopilimeai* to anybody.]

I hope the gentle reader will pardon this digression; but if the gentle reader don't want to do it, he can let it alone.

About half-past eight o'clock a dozen native women rose up and began the sad mourning rites. They locked arms and swayed violently backward and forward; faced around and went through a number of quick gestures with hands, heads and bodies; turned and twisted and mingled together—heads and hands going all the time, and their motions timed to a weird howling which it would be rather complimentary to call singing; and finished up spreading their arms abroad and throwing their heads and bodies far backward simultaneously, and all uttering a deafening squall at the same moment.

'Well, if there's anything between the Farallones and Fiddler's Green as devilish as that, I wish I may—'

'Brown,' I said, 'these solemn and impressive funeral rites of the ancient times have been rescued from the oblivion to which the ignorant missionaries consigned them forty years ago, by the good and wise Lord Bishop Staley, and it ill beseems such as you to speak irreverently of them. I cannot permit you to say more in this vein in my presence.'

When the women had finished the multitude clapped their hands boisterously in token of applause.

A number of native boys next stood up and went through a performance a good deal like that which I have just described, singing, at the same time, a strange, unmusical chant. The audience applauded again. [Harris came out once more on that part of the verandah which could be seen best by the great assemblage, and assumed an attitude and an expression so suggestive of his being burdened with the cares of state of sixty or seventy kingdoms, that, if I had been a stranger, I must have said to myself: 'The trifles Richelieu had to contend with were foolishness to what this man has got on his hands.']

Next, about twenty native women dressed in black rose up and sang some hymns like ours, but in the Kanaka tongue, and made good music of them. Some of the voices were very rich and sweet, the harmony was excellent and the time perfect. Every now and then, while this choir sang (and, in fact, all the evening), old-time natives scattered through the crowd would suddenly break out into a wild heart-broken wail that would almost startle one's pulse into stillness. And there was one old fellow near the center who would get up often, no matter what was going on, and branch forth into a sort of sing-song recitation, which he would eventually change into a stump speech; he seemed to make a good many hits judging by the cordial applause he got from a coterie of admirers in his immediate vicinity.

A dozen men performed next—howled and distorted their bodies and flung their arms fiercely about, like very maniacs.

'God bless my soul, just listen at that racket! Your opinion is your opinion, and I don't quarrel with it; and my opinion is my opinion; and I say, once for all, that if I was Mayor of this town I would just get up here and read the Riot-Act once, if I died for it the next—'

'Brown, I cannot allow this language. These touching expressions of mourning were instituted by the good Bishop, who has come from his English home to teach this poor benighted race to follow the example and imitate the sinless ways of the Redeemer, and did not He mourn for the dead Lazarus? Do not the sacred scriptures say "Jesus wept?"'

I overheard this person Brown muttering something about the imitation being rather overdone or improved on, or something of that kind, but I paid no attention to it. The man means well; his ignorance is his misfortune—not his crime.

Twenty Kanakas in striped knit shirts now filed through the dense crowd and sat down in a double row on the ground; each bore an immense gourd, more than two feet long, with a neck near one end and a head to it; the outer, or largest end, was a foot in diameter; these things were dry and hollow, and are the native tom-toms or drums. Each man set his gourd on end, and supported it with a hand on each side; at a given signal every drummer launched out into a dismal chant and slapped his drum twice in quick succession with his open hands; then three times; then twice again; then—well, I cannot describe it; they slapped the drums in every conceivable way, and the sound produced was as dull and dry as if the drums had been solid stone; then they held them above their heads a few moments, or over their shoulders, or in front of their faces, or behind their necks, and then brought them simultaneously to the ground with a dead, hollow thump; and then they went on slapping them as before. They kept up this most dreary and unexciting performance for twenty minutes or more, and the great concourse of natives watched every motion with rapt and eager admiration, and loudly applauded the musicians.

Brown muttered (under the vile pretense of not intending to be overheard):

'Jesus wept.'

'Brown,' I said, 'your conduct is shameful. It has always been conceded that in following the example set us by the Savior we may be allowed some latitude. But I will not argue with a man who is so bigoted, fault-finding and uncharitable. I will have nothing further to say to you upon this subject.'

'He—He wept.'

I thought I heard those words, but Brown's head was out of the window, and I was not certain. I was already irritated to that degree that to speak would be to lose my temper, and therefore I allowed the suspected mutinous language to pass unnoticed.

After the drumming came the famous hula hula we had heard so much about and so longed to see—the lascivious dance that was wont to set the passions of men ablaze in the old heathen days, a century ago. About thirty buxom young Kanaka women, gayly attired, as I have before remarked, in pink and white, and with heads wreathed with flowers and evergreens, formed themselves into half a dozen rows of five or six in a row, shook the reefs out of their skirts, tightened their girdles and began the most unearthly caterwauling that was ever heard, perhaps; the noise had a marked and regular time to it, however, and they kept strict time to it with writhing bodies; with heads and hands thrust out to the left; then to the right; then a step to the front and the left hands all projected simultaneously forward, and the right hands placed on the hips; then the same repeated with a change of hands; then a mingling together of the performers—quicker time, faster and more violently excited motions—more and more complicated gestures—(the words of their fierce chant meantime treating in broadest terms, and in detail, of things which may be vaguely hinted at in a respectable newspaper, but not distinctly mentioned)—then a convulsive writhing of the person, continued for a few moments and ending in a sudden stop and a grand caterwaul in chorus. [Great applause.]

'Jesus wept.'

I barely heard the words, and that was all. They sounded like blasphemy. I offered no rebuke to the utterer, because I could not disguise from myself that the gentle grief of the Savior was but poorly imitated here—that the heathen orgies resurrected by the Lord Bishop of Honolulu were not warranted by the teachings of the Master whom he professes to serve.

Minister Harris emerging from the palace verandah at this moment with the weight of his sixty kingdoms bearing down on him heavier than ever, and it being past midnight, I judged it time to go home, and I did so.

It is reported that the King has said: 'The foreigners like their religion—let them enjoy it, and freely. But the religion of my fathers is good enough for me.' Now that is all right. At least I think so. And I have no fault to find with the natives for the lingering love they feel for their ancient customs. But I do find fault with Bishop Staley for reviving those customs of a barbarous age at a time when they had long been abandoned and were being forgotten—when one more generation of faithful adherence to the teachings of the American missionaries would have buried them forever and made them memories of the past—things to be talked of and wondered at, like the old laws that made it death for a plebeian to stand erect in the presence of his king, or for a man to speak to his wife on a *tabu* day—but never imitated.

For forty years before the Bishop brought his Royal Hawaiian Established Reformed Catholic Church here the kings and chiefs of this land had been buried with the quiet, simple, Christian rites that are observed in England and America, and no man thought of anything more being necessary. But one of the first things Bishop Staley did when he arrived here a few years ago was to write home that the missionaries had deprived the natives of their innocent sports and pastimes (such as the lascivious hula hula, and the promiscuous bathing in the surf of nude natives of opposite sexes), and one of the next things he did was to attend a hula hula at Waikiki with his holy head tricked out in the flower and evergreen trumpery worn by the hula girls. When the late King died the Bishop revived the half-forgotten howling and hula dancing and other barbarisms in the palace yard, and officiated there as a sort of master of ceremonies. For many a year before he came that wretchedest of all wretched musical abortions, the tom-tom, had not been heard near the heart of Honolulu; but he has reinstated it and brought it into its ancient esteem and popularity. The old superstitions of this people were passing away far faster than is the case with the inhabitants of the unfrequented and sparsely populated country districts of America, France and Wales, but Bishop Staley is putting a stop to progress in this direction.

We owe the strange and unpleasant scenes of last night to him—there are not ten white men in the kingdom who have ever seen their like before in public—and I am told that he is appalled at the work of his own hands—that he is ashamed—that he dreads to think of the comments it will provoke in Christian lands—in a word, that he finds, too late, that he has made a most melancholy blunder.

If I may speak freely, I think this all comes of elevating a weak, trivial-minded man to a position of rank and power—of making a Bishop out of very inferior material—of trying to construct greatness out of constitutional insignificance. My estimate of Bishop Staley is not carelessly formed; there is evidence to back it. He gossips habitually; he lacks the common wisdom to keep still that deadly enemy of a man, his own tongue; he says ill-advised things in public speeches, and then in other public speeches denies that he ever said them; he shows spite, a trait which is not allied to greatness; he is fond of rushing into print, like mediocrity the world over, and is vainer of being my Lord Bishop over a diocese of fifteen thousand men and women (albeit they belong to other people's churches) than some other men would be of wielding the world-wide power of the Pope; and finally, every single important act of his administration has evinced a lack of sagacity and an unripeness of judgment which might be forgiven a youth, but not a full-grown man—or, if that seems too severe, which might be forgiven a restless, visionary nobody, but not a Bishop. My estimate of Bishop Staley may be a wrong one, but it is at least an honest one.

Persons who are intimate with Bishop Staley say he is a good man, and a well educated and cultivated one, and that in social life he is companionable, pleasant and liberal spirited when church matters are not the topic of conversation. This is no doubt true; but it is my province to speak of him in his official, not in his private capacity. He has shown the temerity of an incautious, inexperienced and immature judgment in rushing in here fresh from the heart and home of a high English civilization and throwing down the gauntlet of defiance before a band of stern, tenacious, unyielding, tireless, industrious, devoted old Puritan knights who have seen forty years of missionary service; whose time was never fooled away in theorizing, but whose lightest acts always meant business; who landed here two score years ago, full of that fervent zeal and resistless determination inherited from their Pilgrim forefathers, and marched forth and seized upon this people with a grip of iron, and infused into their being, wrought into their very natures, the spirit of democracy and the religious enthusiasm that animated themselves; whose grip is still upon the race and can never be loosened till they, of their own free will and accord, shall relax it. He showed a marvelous temerity—one weak, inexperienced man against a host of drilled and hardy veterans; and among them great men—men who would be great in wider and broader spheres than that they have chosen here. He miscalculated the force, the confidence, the determination of that Puritan spirit which subdued America and underlies her whole religious fabric to-day—which has subdued these islanders, and whose influence over them can never be unseated.

His church was another miscalculation. It was a mistake to appeal by imposing ceremonies and showy display to a people imbued with a thorough Puritan distaste for such things, and who had never been much accustomed to anything of the kind at any period of their history. There is little in common between the simple evergreen decorations and the tom-toms and hula hulas of the natives, and the cheap magnificence of the Bishop's cathedral altar, his gaudily painted organ-pipes and the monotonous and unattractive ceremonials of his church service.

He is fighting with good nerve, but his side is weak. The moneyed strength of these islands—their agriculture, their commerce, their mercantile affairs—is in the hands of Americans—republicans; the religious power of the country is wielded by Americans—republicans; the whole people are saturated with the spirit of democratic Puritanism, and they are—republicans. This is a *republic*, to the very marrow, and over it sit a King, a dozen Nobles and half a dozen Ministers. The field of the Royal Hawaiian Established Church is thus so circumscribed that the little cathedral in Nuuanu Street, with its thirty pews of ten-individual capacity each, is large enough to accommodate it in its entirety, and have room to spare.

And this is the bugbear that has kept the American missionaries in hot water for three or four years! The Bishop of Honolulu ought to feel flattered that a chance so slim as his, and a power so feeble as his, has been able to accomplish it. But at the same time he ought to feel grateful, because, if let alone, he and his Church must infallibly have been and remained insignificant. I do not say this ill-naturedly, for I bear the Bishop no malice, and I respect his sacred office; I simply state a palpable fact.

I will say a word or two about the Reformed Catholic Church, to the end that strangers may understand its character. Briefly, then, it is a miraculous invention. One might worship this strange production itself without breaking the first commandment, for there is nothing like it in the heavens above or in the earth beneath, or in the water under the earth. The Catholics refuse to accept it as Catholic, the Episcopalians deny that it is the church they are accustomed to, and of course the Puritans claim no kindred with it. It is called a child of the Established Church of England, but it resembles its parent in few particulars. It has got an altar which is gay with fiery velvet, showy white trimmings, vases of flowers and other mantel ornaments. (It was once flanked by imposing, seven-branched candlesticks, but these were obnoxious and have been removed.) Over it is a thing like a gilt sign-board, on which is rudely painted two processions—four personages in each—marching solemnly and in single file toward the crucified Savior in the center, and bringing their baggage with them. The design of it is a secret known only to the artist and his Maker. Near the pulpit is a red canopied shower-bath—I mean it looks like one—upon which is inscribed, 'Separated unto the Gospel of God.' The Bishop sits under it at a small desk, when he has got nothing particular to do. The organ pipes are colored with a ground-work of blue, which is covered all over with a flower-work wrought in other colors. Judging by its striking homeliness, I should say that the artist of the altar-piece had labored here also. Near the door of the church, but inside, of course, stands a small pillar, surmounted by a large shell. It may be for holy water or it may be a contribution box. If the latter be the case, I must protest that this ghastly pun—this mute suggestion to shell out—is ill-suited to the sacred character of the place, and it is only with the profoundest pain that I force myself to even think for a moment upon so distressing a circumstance. Against the wall is a picture of the future Cathedral of Honolulu—a more imposing structure than the present one; that many a year may elapse before it is built is no wish of mine. A dozen acolytes—Chinese, Kanaka and half-white boys, arrayed in white robes, hold positions near the altar, and during the early part of the service they sing and go through some performances suggestive of the regular Catholic services; after that, the majority of the boys go off on furlough. The Bishop reads a chapter from the Bible; then the organist leaves his instrument and sings a litany peculiar to this Church, and not to be heard elsewhere; there is nothing stirring or incendiary about his mild, nasal music; the congregation join the chorus; after this a third clergyman preaches the sermon; these three ecclesiastics all wear white surplices. I have described the evening services. When the Bishop first came here he indulged in a good deal of showy display and ceremony in his Church, but these proved so distasteful, even to Episcopalians, that he shortly modified them very much.

I have spoken rather irreverently once or twice in the above paragraph, and am ashamed of it. But why write it over? I would not be likely to get it any better. I might make the matter worse.

'And say that —'

'Brown, have you, in defiance of all my reproofs, been looking over my shoulder again?'

'Yes, but that's all right, you know—that's all right. Just say—just say that the Bishop works as hard as any man, and makes the best fight he can, and that's a credit to him, anyway.'

'Brown, that is the first charitable sentiment I have ever heard you utter. At a proper moment I will confer upon you a fitting reward for it. But for the present, good-night, son. Go, now. Go to your innocent slumbers. And wash your feet, Brown

—or perhaps it is your teeth—at any rate you are unusually offensive this evening. Remedy the matter. Never mind explaining—good-night.'

The French Roman Catholic Mission here, under the Right Reverend Lord Bishop Maigret, goes along quietly and unostentatiously; and its affairs are conducted with a wisdom which betrays the presence of a leader of distinguished ability. The Catholic clergy are honest, straightforward, frank and open; they are industrious and devoted to their religion and their work; they never meddle; whatever they do can be relied on as being prompted by a good and worthy motive. These things disarm resentment—prejudice cannot exist in their presence. Consequently, Americans are never heard to speak ill or slightingly of the French Catholic Mission. Their religion is not nondescript—it is plain, out and out, undisguised and unmistakable Catholicism. You know right where to find them when you want them. The American missionaries have no quarrel with these men; they honor and respect and esteem them, and bid them God-speed. There is an anomaly for you—Puritan and Roman Catholic striding along, hand in hand, under the banner of the Cross!

Mark Twain

Reprinted from the Sacramento Weekly Union
August 4, 1866.

A ROYAL FUNERAL

July 1, 1866.

AT TEN O'CLOCK yesterday morning, the court, members of the Legislature and various diplomatic bodies assembled at the Iolani Palace, to be present at the funeral of the late Princess. The sermon was preached by the Rev. Mr. Parker, pastor of the great stone church—of which the Princess was a member, I believe, and whose choir she used to lead in the days of her early womanhood. To the day of her death she was a staunch, unwavering friend and ally of the missionaries, and it is a matter of no surprise that Parker, always eloquent, spoke upon this occasion with a feeling and pathos which visibly moved the hearts of men accustomed to conceal their emotions.

The Bishop of Honolulu, ever zealous, had sought permission to officiate in Parker's stead, but after duly considering the fact that the Princess had always regarded the Bishop with an unfriendly eye and had persistently refused to have anything to do with his church, his request was denied. However, he demanded and was granted the place of honor in the procession, although it belonged properly to the officiating clergyman. The Bishop also claimed that inasmuch as the Royal Mausoleum was consecrated ground, it would be sacrilegious to allow a Calvinistic minister to officiate there when the body was consigned to the tomb, and so he was allowed to conduct that portion of the obsequies himself. However, he explained that it was not the custom of his church to read a burial service or offer up a prayer over such as had never belonged to that church, and therefore the departed Princess was consigned to her last resting-place with no warmer or kindlier a recommendation than a meager, noncommittal benediction—a sort of chilly funereal politeness—nothing more. But then we should not blame the Bishop in this matter, because he has both authority and example to sustain his position, as I find by reference to a 'Review' by W. D. Alexander of one of his 'Pastoral Addresses.' I quote from Alexander:

'Only last December, Thomas Powell, near Peterborough, in England, wished to have his son buried in the parish churchyard, and a Dissenting minister to officiate. When the friends had gathered around the grave, a messenger arrived from the clergyman of the Established Church, one Ellaby, stating that he was ready to perform the Episcopal service. This was courteously declined, upon which the Rector issued from the church and forbade the burial. Even the right of silent interment was denied them, and when the afflicted father would himself perform the last sad offices at the grave of his child, the spade was wrenched from his hand by the sexton.'

In offering this defense of the Bishop of Honolulu, I do so simply with an unselfish wish to do him justice and save him from hasty and injurious criticism, and *not* through a mean desire to curry favor with him.

As the hour of eleven approached, large bodies of white and

native residents, chiefly on horseback, moved toward the palace through the quiet streets, to see the procession form. All business houses were closed, of course, and many a flag, half-mast high, swung lazily in the Summer air.

The procession began to move at eleven, amid the solemn tolling of bells and the dull booming of minute guns from the heights overlooking the city. A glance of the eye down the procession revealed a striking and picturesque spectacle—large bodies of women, in melancholy black, and roofed over with a far-reaching double line of black umbrellas; troops of men and children, in black; carriages, with horses clad from head to foot in sable velvet; and in strong contrast with all this were the bright colors flashing here and there along the pageant—swarthy Zouaves, in crimson raiment; soldiers, in blue and white and other lively hues; mounted lancers, with red and white pennants fluttering from their weapons; nobles and great officers in splendid uniforms; and—conspicuous amid its gloomy surroundings—the catafalque, flanked on either side with gorgeously-tinted kahilis. The slow and measured tread of the marching squadrons; the mournful music of the bands; the chanting of the virtues of the dead and the warrior deeds of her ancestors, by a gray and venerable woman here and there; the wild wail that rang out at times from some bereaved one to whom the occasion brought back the spirit of the buried past—these completed the effect.

The kahilis are symbols of mourning which are sacred to the aristocracy. They are immense plumes, mounted upon tall poles, and are made of feathers of all bright and beautiful colors; some are a rich purple; some crimson; others brown, blue, white and black, etc. These are all dyed, but the costly kahilis formed of the yellow feather of royalty (*tabu* to the common herd) were tinted by the hand of nature, and come from the tropic bird, which, as I have said in a previous letter, has but two of them—one under each wing. One or two kahilis, also, made of red feathers from a bird called by sailors the marlinespike bird, had no artificial coloring about them. These feathers are very long and slender (hence the fowl's name), and each bird's tail is furnished with two, and only two, of them. The birds of the Sandwich Islands seem uncommonly indigent in the matter of strictly ornamental feathers. A dozen or more of these gaudy kahilis were upheld by pall-bearers of high blood and fenced in the stately catafalque with a vari-colored wall as brilliant as a rainbow. Through the arches of the catafalque could be seen the coffin, draped with that badge and symbol of royalty, the famous yellow-feather war-cloak, whose construction occupied the toiling hands of its manufacturers during nine generations of Hawaiian Kings.

We have here, in this little land of 50,000 inhabitants, the complete machinery, in its minutest details, of a vast and imposing empire, done in miniature. We have all the sounding titles, all the grades and castes, all the pomp and circumstance, of a great monarchy. To the curious, the following published programme of the procession will not be uninteresting. After reading the long list of dignitaries, etc., and remembering the sparseness of the population, one is almost inclined to wonder where the material for that portion of the procession devoted to 'Hawaiian Population Generally' is going to be procured:

UNDERTAKER.

ROYAL SCHOOL. KAWAIAHAO SCHOOL. ROMAN CATHOLIC SCHOOL.

MAEMAE SCHOOL.

HONOLULU FIRE DEPARTMENT.

MECHANICS' BENEFIT UNION.

ATTENDING PHYSICIANS.

KONOHIKIS (SUPERINTENDENTS) OF THE CROWN LANDS,

KONOHIKIS OF THE PRIVATE LANDS OF HIS MAJESTY,

KONOHIKIS OF PRIVATE LANDS OF HER LATE ROYAL HIGHNESS.

GOVERNOR OF OAHU AND STAFF.

HULUMANU (MILITARY COMPANY).

THE PRINCE OF HAWAII'S OWN (MILITARY COMPANY).

HOUSEHOLD TROOPS.

THE KING'S HOUSEHOLD SERVANTS.

SERVANTS OF HER LATE ROYAL HIGHNESS.

PROTESTANT CLERGY. THE CLERGY OF THE ROMAN CATHOLIC CHURCH.

HIS LORDSHIP LOUIS MAIGRET,

THE RIGHT REV. BISHOP OF ARATHEA,

VICAR-APOSTOLIC OF THE HAWAIIAN ISLANDS.

THE CLERGY OF THE HAWAIIAN REFORMED CATHOLIC CHURCH.

HIS LORDSHIP THE RIGHT REV. BISHOP OF HONOLULU.

ESCORT HAWAIIAN CAVALRY.	LARGE KAHILIS.	SMALL KAHILIS.	PALL-BEARERS.	[HEARSE.]	PALL-BEARERS.	SMALL KAHILIS.	LARGE KAHILIS.	ESCORT HAWAIIAN CAVALRY.

HER MAJESTY QUEEN EMMA'S CARRIAGE.

HIS MAJESTY'S STAFF.

CARRIAGE OF HER LATE ROYAL HIGHNESS.

CARRIAGE OF HER MAJESTY THE QUEEN DOWAGER.

THE KING'S CHANCELLOR.

CABINET MINISTERS.

HIS EXCELLENCY THE MINISTER RESIDENT OF THE UNITED STATES,

JAMES MCBRIDE.

H. I. M.'S COMMISSIONER, MONS. DESNOYERS.

H. B. M.'S ACTING COMMISSIONER, W. L. GREEN.

JUDGES OF SUPREME COURT.

PRIVY COUNCILLORS,

MEMBERS OF LEGISLATIVE ASSEMBLY.

CONSULAR CORPS.

CIRCUIT JUDGES.

CLERKS OF GOVERNMENT DEPARTMENTS.

MEMBERS OF THE BAR.

COLLECTOR GENERAL, CUSTOM-HOUSE OFFICERS AND OFFICERS OF THE CUSTOMS.

MARSHAL AND SHERIFFS OF THE DIFFERENT ISLANDS.

KING'S YEOMANRY.

FOREIGN RESIDENTS.

AHAHUI KAAHUMANU.

HAWAIIAN POPULATION GENERALLY.

HAWAIIAN CAVALRY.

POLICE FORCE.

The 'Ahahui Kaahumanu'—a benevolent society instituted (and presided over) by the late Princess for the nursing of the sick and the burial of the dead—was numerously represented. It is composed solely of native women. They were dressed in black, and wore sashes of different colors.

His Majesty the King, attended by a guard of nobles and princes, whose uniforms were splendid, with bright colors and loops and braids of gold, rode with his venerable father in the first carriage in the rear of the catafalque. The Bishop of Honolulu occupied the place of honor in that portion of the procession which preceded the catafalque.

The servants of the King and the late Princess would have made quite a respectable procession by themselves. They numbered two hundred and fifty, perhaps.

Four or five poodle dogs, which had been the property of the deceased, were carried in the arms of individuals among these servants of peculiar and distinguished trustworthiness. It is likely that all the Christianity the Hawaiians could absorb would never be sufficient to wean them from their almost idolatrous affection for dogs. And these dogs, as a general thing, are the smallest, meanest, and most spiritless, homely and contemptible of their species.

As the procession passed along the broad and beautiful Nuuanu Street, an innocent native would step out occasionally from the ranks, procure a slice of watermelon, or a pineapple, or a lighted pipe, from some dusky spectator and return to his place and enjoy the refreshing luxury as he kept step with the melancholy music.

When we had thoroughly examined the pageant we retired to a back street and galloped ahead to the mausoleum, two miles from the center of the town, and sat down to wait. This mausoleum is a neat edifice, built of dressed blocks of coral; has a high, sharp, slated roof, and its form is that of a Greek cross. The remains of the later Kings repose in it, but those of ancient times were hidden or burned, in compliance with a custom of the dark ages; some say, to prevent evil-disposed persons from getting hold of them and thus being enabled to pray a descendant to death; others say, to prevent the natives from making fishhooks out of them, it being held that there were superior fishhook virtues in the bones of a high chief. There are other theories for accounting for this custom, but I have forgotten what they are. It is said that it was usual to send a friend to hide the bones (after they had been stripped of the flesh and neatly tied in a bundle), and then waylay him and kill him as he came back, whereby it will be observed that to do a favor of this kind was attended with consequences which could not be otherwise than disagreeable to the party assuming the kindly office of undertaker to a dead dignitary. Of course, as you will easily divine, the man was killed to prevent the possibility of his divulging his precious secret.

The mausoleum is large enough to accommodate many dead Kings and Princes. It stands in the middle of a large grass-clad lawn, which is inclosed by a stone wall.

As the procession filed through the gate, the military deployed handsomely to the right and left and formed an avenue through which the long column of mourners passed to the tomb. The coffin was borne through the door of the mausoleum, followed by the King and his chiefs, the great officers of the kingdom, foreign Consuls, Embassadors and distinguished guests (Burlingame and General Van Valkenburgh). Several of the kahilis were then fastened to a frame-work in front of the tomb, there to remain until they decay and fall to pieces, or, forestalling this, until another scion of royalty dies. At this point of the proceedings the multitude set up such a dismal, heart-broken wailing as I hope never to hear again. The soldiers fired three volleys of musketry—the wailing being previously silenced to permit of the guns being heard. His Highness Prince William, in a showy military uniform (who was formerly betrothed to the Princess but was not allowed to marry her), stood guard and paced back and forth within the door. The privileged few who followed the coffin into the mausoleum remained some time, but the King soon came out and stood in the door and near one side of it. A stranger could have guessed his rank (although he was so simply and unpretentiously dressed) by the profound deference paid him by all persons in his vicinity; by seeing his high officers receive his quiet orders and suggestions with bowed and uncovered heads; and by observing how careful those persons who came out of the mausoleum were to avoid 'crowding' him (although there was room enough in the doorway for a wagon to pass, for that matter); how respectfully they edged out sideways, scraping their backs against the wall and always presenting a front view of their persons to His Majesty, and never putting their hats on until they were well out of the royal presence.

The King is thirty-four years of age, it is said, but looks all of fifty. He has an observant, inquiring eye, a heavy, massive face, a lighter complexion than is common with his race, tolerably short, stiff hair, a moderate mustache and imperial, large stature, inclining somewhat to corpulence (I suppose he weighs fully one hundred and eighty—may be a little over), has fleshy hands, but a small foot for his size, is about six feet high, is thoughtful and slow of movement, has a large head, firmly set upon broad shoulders, and is a better man and a better looking one than he is represented to be in the villainous popular photographs of him, for none of them are good. That last remark is surplusage, however, for no photograph ever was good, yet, of anybody—hunger and thirst and utter wretchedness overtake the outlaw who invented it! It transforms into desperadoes the meekest of men; depicts sinless innocence upon the pictured faces of ruffians; gives the wise man the stupid leer of a fool, and a fool an expression of more than earthly wisdom. If a man tries to look merely serious when he sits for his picture, the photograph makes him as solemn as an owl; if he smiles, the photograph smirks repulsively; if he tries to look pleasant, the photograph looks silly; if he makes the fatal mistake of attempting to seem pensive, the camera will surely write him down an ass. The sun never looks through the photographic instrument that it does not print a lie. The piece of glass it prints it on is well named a 'negative'—a contradiction—a misrepresentation—a falsehood. I speak feelingly of this matter, because by turns the instrument has represented me to be a lunatic, a Solomon, a missionary, a burglar and an abject idiot, and I am neither.

The King was dressed entirely in black—dress-coat and silk hat—and looked rather democratic in the midst of the showy uniforms about him. On his breast he wore a large gold star, which was half hidden by the lappel of his coat. He remained at the door a half hour, and occasionally gave an order to the men who were erecting the kahilis before the tomb. He had the good taste to make one of them substitute black crape for the ordinary hempen rope he was about to tie one of them to the framework with. Finally he entered his carriage and drove away, and the populace shortly began to drop in his wake. While he was in view there was but one man who attracted more attention than himself, and that was Minister Harris. This feeble personage had crape enough around his hat to express the grief of an entire nation, and as usual he neglected no opportunity of making himself conspicuous and exciting the admiration of the simple Kanakas. Oh! noble ambition of this modern Richelieu!

It is interesting to contrast the funeral ceremonies of the Princess Victoria with those of her great ancestor Kamehameha the Conqueror, who died less than fifty years ago—in 1819, the year before the first missionaries came:

'On the 8th of May, 1819, at the age of sixty-six, he died, as he had lived, in the faith of his country. It was his misfortune not to have come in contact with men who could have rightly influenced his religious aspirations. Judged by his advantages and compared with the most eminent of his countrymen he may be justly styled not only great, but good. To this day his memory warms the heart and elevates the national feelings of Hawaiians. They are proud of their old warrior King; they love his name; his deeds form their historical age; and an enthusiasm everywhere prevails, shared even by foreigners who knew his worth, that constitutes the firmest pillar of the throne of his son.

'In lieu of human victims (the custom of that age), a sacrifice of three hundred dogs attended his obsequies—no mean holocaust when their national value and the estimation in which they were held are considered. The bones of Kamehameha, after being kept for a while, were so carefully concealed that all knowledge of their final resting-place is now lost. There was a proverb current among the common people that the bones of a cruel King could not be hid; they made fish-hooks and arrows of them, upon which, in using them, they vented their abhorrence of his memory in bitter execrations.'

The account of the circumstances of his death, as written by the native historians, is full of minute detail, but there is scarcely a line of it which does not mention or illustrate some by-gone custom of the country. In this respect it is the most comprehensive document I have yet met with. I will quote it entire:

'When Kamehameha was dangerously sick and the priests were unable to cure him, they said: "Be of good courage and build a house for the god" (his own private god or idol) "that thou mayest recover." The chiefs corroborated this advice of the priests, and a place of worship was prepared for Kukailimoku, and consecrated in the evening. They proposed also to the King, with a view to prolong his life, that human victims should be sacrificed to his deity; upon which the greater part of the people absconded through fear of death, and concealed themselves in hiding-places till the *tabu*, in which destruction impended, was past. It is doubtful whether Kamehameha approved of the plan of the chiefs and priests to sacrifice men, as he was known to say, "The men are sacred for the King;" meaning that they were for the service of his successor. This information was derived from Liholiho, his son.

'After this, his sickness increased to such a degree that he had not strength to turn himself in his bed. When another season, consecrated for worship at the new temple (*heiau*) arrived, he said to his son, Liholiho, "Go thou and make supplication to thy god; I am not able to go, and will offer my prayers at home." When his devotions to his feathered god, Kukailimoku, were concluded, a certain religiously disposed individual, who had a bird god, suggested to the King that through its influence his sickness might be removed. The name of this god was Pua; its body was made of a bird, now eaten by the Hawaiians, and called in their language *alae*. Kamehameha was willing that a trial should be made, and two houses were constructed to facilitate the experiment; but while dwelling in them he became so very weak as not to receive food. After lying there three days, his wives, children and chiefs, perceiving that he was very low, returned him to his own house. In the evening he was carried to the eating-house, where he took a little food in his mouth which he did not swallow; also a cup of water. The chiefs requested him to give them his counsel; but he made no reply, and was carried back to the dwelling-house; but when near midnight—ten o'clock, perhaps—he was carried again to the place to eat; but, as before, he merely tasted of what was presented to him. Then Kaikioewa addressed him thus: "Here we all are, your younger brethren, your son Liholiho and your foreigner; impart to us your dying charge, that Liholiho and Kaahumanu may hear." Then Kamehameha inquired, "What do you say?" Kaikioewa repeated, "Your counsels for us." He then said, "Move on in my good way and—" He could proceed no further. The foreigner, Mr. Young, embraced and kissed him. Hoapili also embraced him, whispering something in his ear, after which he was taken back to the house. About twelve he was carried once more to the house for eating, into which his head entered, while his body was in the dwelling-house immediately adjoining. It should be remarked that this frequent carrying of a sick chief from one house to another resulted from the *tabu* system, then in force. There were at that time six houses connected with an establishment—one was for worship, one for the men to eat in, an eating-house for the women, a house to sleep in, a house in which to manufacture kapa (native cloth) and one where, at certain intervals, the women might dwell in seclusion.

'The sick was once more taken to his house, when he expired; this was at two o'clock, a circumstance from which Leleiohoku derived his name. As he breathed his last, Kalaimoku came to the eating-house to order those in it to go out. There were two aged persons thus directed to depart; one went, the other remained on account of love to the King, by whom he had formerly been kindly sustained. The children also were sent away. Then Kalaimoku came to the house, and the chiefs had a consultation. One of them spoke thus: "This is my thought—we will eat him raw." Kaahumanu (one of the dead King's widows) replied, "Perhaps his body is not at our disposal; that is more properly with his successor. Our part in him—his breath—has departed; his remains will be disposed of by Liholiho."

'After this conversation the body was taken into the consecrated house for the performance of the proper rites by the priest and the new King. The name of this ceremony is *uko*; and when the sacred hog was baked the priest offered it to the dead body, and it became a god, the King at the same time repeating the customary prayers.

'Then the priest, addressing himself to the King and chiefs, said: "I will now make known to you the rules to be observed respecting persons to be sacrificed on the burial of this body. If you obtain one man before the corpse is removed, one will be sufficient; but after it leaves this house four will be required. If delayed until we carry the corpse to the grave there must be ten; but after it is deposited in the grave there must be fifteen. To-morrow morning there will be a *tabu*, and, if the sacrifice be delayed until that time, forty men must die."

'Then the high priest, Hewahewa, inquired of the chiefs, "Where shall be the residence of King Liholiho?" They replied, "Where, indeed? You, of all men, ought to know." Then the priest observed, "There are two suitable places; one is Kau, the other is Kohala." The chiefs preferred the latter, as it was more thickly inhabited. The priest added, "These are proper places for the King's residence; but he must not remain in Kona, for it is polluted." This was agreed to. It was now break of day. As he was being carried to the place of burial the people perceived that their King was dead, and they wailed. When the corpse was removed from the house to the tomb, a distance of one chain, the procession was met by a certain man who was ardently attached to the deceased. He leaped upon the chiefs who were carrying the King's body; he desired to die with him on account of his love. The chiefs drove him away. He persisted in making numerous attempts, which were unavailing. Kalaimoku also had it in his heart to die with him, but was prevented by Hookio.

'The morning following Kamehameha's death, Liholiho and his train departed for Kohala, according to the suggestion of the priest, to avoid the defilement occasioned by the dead. At this time if a chief died the land was polluted, and the heirs sought a residence in another part of the country until the corpse was dissected and the bones tied in a bundle, which being done, the season of defilement terminated. If the deceased were not a chief, the house only was defiled, which became pure again on the burial of the body. Such were the laws on this subject.

'On the morning on which Liholiho sailed in his canoe for Kohala, the chiefs and people mourned after their manner on occasion of a chief's death, conducting themselves like madmen and like beasts. Their conduct was such as to forbid description. The priests, also, put into action the sorcery apparatus, that the person who had prayed the King to death might die; for it was not believed that Kamehameha's departure was the effect either of sickness or old age. When the sorcerers set up by their fire-places sticks with a strip of kapa flying at the top, the chief Keeaumoku, Kaahumanu's brother, came in a state of intoxication and broke the flagstaff of the sorcerers, from which it was inferred that Kaahumanu and her friends had been instrumental in the King's death. On this account they were subjected to abuse.'

You have the contrast, now, and a strange one it is. This great Queen, Kaahumanu, who was 'subjected to abuse' during the frightful orgies that followed the King's death, in accordance with ancient custom, afterwards became a devout Christian and a steadfast and powerful friend of the missionaries.

MARK TWAIN

Burlingame and Van Valkenburgh, United States Ministers to China and Japan, are ready to sail, but are delayed by the absence of two attaches, who went to Hawaii to see the volcano, and who were not aware how slow a country this is to get around in. The journey hence to Hilo, which would be made anywhere else almost in eighteen or twenty hours, requires a week in the little inter-island schooners.

Colonel Kalakaua, the King's Chamberlain, has invited the Ministerial party to a great *luau* (native dinner) at Waikiki.

Gen. Van Valkenburgh has achieved a distinguished success as a curiosity-finder—not hunter. Standing on the celebrated

Pari, a day or two ago, and amusing himself by idly punching into the compact lava wall through which the road is cut, he crumbled away a chunk of it, and observing something white sticking to it, he instituted an examination, and found a sound, white, unmarred and unblemished human jaw-tooth firmly imbedded in the lava! Now the question is, how did it get there—in the side (where a road had been cut in) of a mountain of lava—seven hundred feet above the valley? a mountain which has been there for ages, this being one of the oldest islands in the group. Burlingame was present and saw the General unearth his prize. I have critically examined it, but, as I half expected myself, the world knows as much about how to account for the wonder now as if I had let it alone. In old times, the bones of chiefs were often thrown into the volcanoes, to make sure that no enemy could get a chance to meddle with them; and Brown has given it as his deliberate opinion that 'that old snag used to belong to one of them fellows.' Possibly—but the opinion comes from a source which entitles it to but little weight. However, that tooth is as notable a curiosity as any I have yet seen in the Sandwich Islands.

M.T.

Reprinted from the Sacramento Weekly Union
August 4, 1866.

AT SEA AGAIN

July —
1866.

BOUND for Hawaii, to visit the great volcano and behold the other notable things which distinguish this island above the remainder of the group, we sailed from Honolulu on a certain Saturday afternoon, in the good schooner *Boomerang*.

The *Boomerang* was about as long as two street cars, and about as wide as one. She was so small (though she was larger than the majority of the inter-island coasters) that when I stood on her deck I felt but little smaller than the Colossus of Rhodes must have felt when he had a man-of-war under him. I could reach the water when she lay over under a strong breeze. When the Captain and Brown and myself and four other gentlemen and the wheelsman were all assembled on the little after portion of the deck which is sacred to the cabin passengers, it was full—there was not room for any more quality folks. Another section of the deck, twice as large as ours, was full of natives of both sexes, with their customary dogs, mats, blankets, pipes, calabashes of poi, fleas, and other luxuries and baggage of minor importance. As soon as we set sail the natives all laid down on the deck as thick as negroes in a slave-pen, and smoked and conversed and captured vermin and eat them, spit on each other, and were truly sociable.

The little low-ceiled cabin below was rather larger than a hearse, and as dark as a vault. It had two coffins on each side—I mean two bunks—though Mr. Brown, with that spirit of irreverence which is so sad a feature of his nature, preferred to call the bunk he was allotted his shelf. A small table, capable of accommodating three persons at dinner, stood against the forward bulkhead, and over it hung the dingiest whale-oil lantern that ever peopled the obscurity of a dungeon with grim and ghostly shapes. The floor room unoccupied was not extensive. One might swing a cat in it, perhaps, but then it would be fatal to the cat to do it. The hold forward of the bulkhead had but little freight in it, and from morning till night a villainous old rooster, with a voice like Baalam's ass, and the same disposition to use it, strutted up and down in that part of the vessel and crowed. He usually took dinner at six o'clock, and then, after an hour devoted to meditation, he mounted a barrel and crowed a good part of the night. He got hoarser and hoarser all the time, but he scorned to allow any personal consideration to interfere with his duty, and kept up his labors in defiance of threatened diphtheria.

Sleeping was out of the question when he was on watch. He was a source of genuine aggravation and annoyance to me. It was worse than useless to shout at him or apply offensive epithets to him—he only took these things for applause, and strained himself to make more noise. Occasionally, during the day, I threw potatoes at him through an aperture in the bulkhead, but he simply dodged them and went on crowing.

The first night, as I lay in my coffin, idly watching the dim lamp swinging to the rolling of the ship, and snuffing the nauseous odors of bilge-water, I felt something gallop over me. Lazarus did not come out of his sepulchre with a more cheerful alacrity than I did out of mine. However, I turned in again when I found it was only a rat. Presently something galloped over me once more. I knew it was not a rat this time, and I thought it might be a centipede, because the Captain had killed one on deck in the afternoon. I turned out. The first glance at the pillow showed me a repulsive sentinel perched upon each end of it—cockroaches as large as peach leaves—fellows with long, quivering antennæ and fiery, malignant eyes. They were grating their teeth like tobacco worms, and appeared to be dissatisfied about something. I had often heard that these reptiles were in the habit of eating off sleeping sailors' toe-nails down to the quick, and I would not get in the bunk any more. I laid down on the floor. But a rat came and bothered me, and shortly afterward a procession of cockroaches arrived and camped in my hair. In a few moments the rooster was crowing with uncommon spirit and a party of fleas were throwing double summersets about my person in the wildest disorder, and taking a bite every time they struck. I was beginning to feel really annoyed. I got up and put my clothes on and went on deck.

The above is not an attempt to be spicy; it is simply an attempt to give a truthful sketch of inter-island schooner life. There is no such thing as keeping a vessel in elegant condition, I think, when she carries molasses and Kanakas.

It was compensation for all my sufferings to come unexpectedly upon so beautiful a scene as met my eye—to step suddenly out of the sepulchral gloom of the cabin and stand under the strong light of the moon—in the center, as it were, of a glittering sea of liquid silver, to see the broad sails straining in the gale, the ship keeled over on her side, the angry foam hissing past her lee bulwarks, and sparkling sheets of spray dashing high over her bows and raining upon her decks; to brace myself and hang fast to the first object that presented itself, with hat jammed down and coat tails whipping in the breeze, and feel that exhilaration that thrills in one's hair and quivers down his back-bone when he knows that every inch of canvas is drawing and the vessel cleaving through the billows at her utmost speed. There was no darkness, no dimness, no obscurity there. All was brightness, every object was vividly defined. Every prostrate Kanaka; every coil of rope; every calabash of poi; every puppy; every seam in the flooring; every bolthead; every object, however minute, showed sharp and distinct in its every outline; and the shadow of the broad mainsail lay black as a pall upon the deck, leaving Brown's white upturned face glorified and his body in a total eclipse.

I turned to look down upon the sparkling animalculæ of the South Seas and watch the train of jeweled fire they made in the wake of the vessel. I—

'Oh, me!'

'What is the matter, Brown?'

'Oh, me!'

'You said that before, Brown. Such tautology—'

'Tautology be hanged! This is no time to talk to a man about tautology when he is sick—so sick—oh, my! and has vomited up his heart and—ah, me—oh hand me that soup dish, and don't stand there hanging to that bulkhead looking like a fool!'

I handed him an absurd tin shaving-pot, called 'berth-pan,' which they hang by a hook to the edge of a berth for the use of distressed landsmen with unsettled stomachs, but all the sufferer's efforts were fruitless—his tortured stomach refused to yield up its cargo.

I do not often pity this bitter enemy to sentiment—he would not thank me for it, anyhow—but now I did pity him; and I pitied him from the bottom of my heart. Any man with any feeling, must have been touched to see him in such misery. I did not try to help him—indeed I did not even think of so unpromising a thing—but I sat down by him to talk to him and so cause the tedious hours to pass less wearily, if possible. I talked to him for some time, but strangely enough, pathetic narratives did not move his emotions, eloquent declamation did not inspirit him, and the most humerous anecdotes failed to make him even smile. He seemed as distressed and restless, at intervals—albeit the rule of his present case was to seem to look like an allegory of unconditional surrender—hopeless, helpless and indifferent—he seemed as distressed and restless as if my conversation and my anecdotes were irksome to him. It was because of this that at last I dropped into poetry. I said I had been writing a poem—or rather, been paraphrasing a passage in Shakespeare—a passage full of wisdom, which I thought I might remember easier if I reduced it to rhyme—hoped it would be pleasant to him—said I had taken but few liberties with the original; had preserved its brevity and terseness, its language as nearly as possible, and its ideas in their regular sequence—and proceeded to read it to him, as follows:

POLONIUS' ADVICE TO HIS SON—PARAPHRASED FROM HAMLET

Beware of the spoken word! Be wise;
Bury thy thoughts in thy breast;
Nor let thoughts that are unnatural
Be ever in acts expressed.

Be thou courteous and kindly toward all—
Be familiar and vulgar with none;
But the friends thou hast proved in thy need,
Hold thou fast till life's mission is done!

Shake not thy faith by confiding
In every new-begot friend,
Beware thou of quarrels—but, in them,
Fight them out to the bitter end.

Give thine ear unto all that would seek it,
But to few thy voice impart;
Receive and consider all censure,
But thy judgment seal in thy heart.

Let thy habit be ever as costly
As thy purse is able to span;
Never gaudy, but rich—for the raiment
Full often proclaimeth the man.

Neither borrow nor lend—oft a loan
Both loseth itself and a friend,
And to borrow relaxeth the thrift
Whereby husbandry gaineth its end.

But lo! above all set this law:
UNTO THYSELF BE THOU TRUE!
Then never toward any canst thou
The deed of a false heart do.

As I finished, Brown's stomach cast up its contents, and in a minute or two he felt entirely relieved and comfortable. He then said that the anecdotes and the eloquence were 'no good,' but if he got seasick again he would like some more poetry.

Monday morning we were close to the island of Hawaii. Two of its high mountains were in view—Mauna Loa and Hualalai. The latter is an imposing peak, but being only ten thousand feet high is seldom mentioned or heard of. Mauna Loa is fourteen thousand feet high. The rays of glittering snow and ice, that clasped its summit like a claw, looked refreshing when viewed from the blistering climate we were in. One could stand on that mountain (wrapped up in blankets and furs to keep warm), and while he nibbled a snow-ball or an icicle to quench his thirst he could look down the long sweep of its sides and see spots where plants are growing that grow only where the bitter cold of Winter prevails; lower down he could see sections devoted to productions that thrive in the temperate zone alone; and at the bottom of the mountain he could see the home of the tufted cocoa-palms and other species of vegetation that grow only in the sultry atmosphere of eternal Summers. He could see all the climes of the world at a single glance of the eye, and that glance would only pass over a distance of eight or ten miles as the bird flies.

We landed at Kailua (pronounced Ki-loo-ah), a little collection of native grass houses reposing under tall cocoa-nut trees—the sleepiest, quietest, Sundayest looking place you can imagine. Ye weary ones that are sick of the labor and care, and the bewildering turmoil of the great world, and sigh for a land where ye may fold your tired hands and slumber your lives peacefully away, pack up your carpet-sacks and go to Kailua! A week there ought to cure the saddest of you all.

An old ruin of lava-block walls down by the sea was pointed out as a fort built by John Adams for Kamehameha I, and mounted with heavy guns—some of them 32-pounders—by the same sagacious Englishman. I was told the fort was dismantled a few years ago, and the guns sold in San Francisco for old iron—which was very improbable. I was told that an adjacent ruin was old Kamehameha's sleeping-house; another, his eating-house; another, his god's house; another, his wife's eating-house—for by the ancient *tabu* system, it was death for man and woman to eat together. Every married man's premises comprised five or six houses. This was the law of the land. It was this custom, no doubt, which has left every pleasant valley in these islands marked with the ruins of numerous house inclosures, and given strangers the impression that the population must have been vast before those houses were deserted; but the argument loses much of its force when you come to consider that the houses absolutely necessary for half a dozen married men were sufficient in themselves to form one of the deserted 'villages' so frequently pointed out to the 'Californian' (to the natives all whites are *haoles*—how-ries—that is, strangers, or, more properly, foreigners; and to the white residents all white new comers are 'Californians'—the term is used more for convenience than anything else).

I was told, also, that Kailua was old Kamehameha's favorite place of residence, and that it was always a favorite place of resort with his successors. Very well, if Kailua suits these kings—all right. Every man to his taste; but, as Brown observed in this connection, 'You'll excuse *me*.'

I was told a good many other things concerning Kailua—not one of which interested me in the least. I was weary and worn with the plunging of the *Boomerang* in the always stormy passages between the islands; I was tired of hanging on by my teeth and toe-nails; and, above all, I was tired of stewed chicken. All I wanted was an hour's rest on a foundation that would let me stand up straight without running any risk—but no information; I wanted something to eat that was not stewed chicken—I didn't care what—but no information. I took no notes, and had no inclination to take any.

Now, the foregoing is nothing but the feverish irritability of a short, rough sea-voyage coming to the surface—a voyage so short that it affords no time for you to tone down and grow quiet and reconciled, and get your stomach in order, and the bad taste out of your mouth, and the unhealthy coating off your tongue.

I snarled at the old rooster and the cockroaches and the national stewed chicken all the time—not because these troubles could be removed, but only because it was a sanitary necessity to snarl at something or perish. One's salt-water spleen must be growled out of the system—there is no other relief. I pined—I longed—I yearned to growl at the Captain himself, but there was no opening. The man had had such passengers before, I suppose, and knew how to handle them, and so he was polite and painstaking and accommodating—and most exasperatingly patient and even-tempered. So I said to myself 'I will take it out of your old schooner, anyhow; I will blackguard the *Boomerang* in the public prints, to pay for your shameless good-nature when your passengers are peevish and actually need somebody to growl at for very relief! '

But now that I am restored by the land breeze, I wonder at my ingratitude; for no man ever treated me better than Captain Kangaroo did on board his ship. As for the stewed chicken—that last and meanest substitute for something to eat—that soothing rubbish for toothless infants—that diet for cholera patients in the rice-water stage—it was of course about the best food we could have at sea, and so I only abused it because I hated it as I do sardines or tomatoes, and because it was stewed chicken and because it was such a relief to abuse somebody or something. But Kangaroo—I never abused Captain Kangaroo. I hope I have a better heart than to abuse a man who, with the kindest and most generous and unselfish motive in the world, went into the galley, and with his own hands baked for me the worst piece of bread I ever ate in my life. His motive was good, his desire to help me was sincere, but his execution was damnable. You see, I was not sick, but nothing would taste good to me; the Kanaka cook's bread was particularly unpalatable; he was a new hand—the regular cook being sick and helpless below—and Captain Kangaroo, in the genuine goodness of his heart, felt for me in my distress and went down and made that most infernal bread. I ate one of those rolls—I would have eaten it if it had killed me—and said to myself: 'It is on my stomach; 'tis well; if it were on my conscience, life would be a burden to me.' I carried one up to Brown and he ate a piece, but declined to experiment further. I insisted, but he said no, he didn't want any more ballast. When the good deeds of men are judged in the Great Day that is to bring bliss or eternal woe to us all, the charity that was in Captain Kangaroo's heart will be remembered and rewarded, albeit his bread will have been forgotten for ages.

It was only about fifteen miles from Kailua to Kealakekua Bay, either by sea or by land, but by the former route there was a point to be weathered where the ship would be the sport of contrary winds for hours, and she would probably occupy the entire day in making the trip, whereas we could do it on horseback in a little while and have the cheering benefit of a respite from the discomforts we had been experiencing on the vessel. We hired horses from the Kanakas, and miserable affairs they were, too. They had lived on meditation all their lives, no doubt, for Kailua is fruitful in nothing else. I will mention, in this place, that horses are plenty everywhere in the Sandwich Islands—no Kanaka is without one or more—but when you travel from one island to another, it is necessary to take your own saddle and bridle, for these articles are scarce. It is singular baggage for a sea voyage, but it will not do to go without it.

The ride through the district of Kona to Kealakekua Bay took us through the famous coffee and orange section. I think the Kona coffee has a richer flavor than any other, be it grown where it may and call it by what name you please. At one time it was cultivated quite extensively, and promised to become one of the great staples of Hawaiian commerce; but the heaviest crop ever raised was almost entirely destroyed by a blight, and this, together with heavy American customs' duties, had the effect of suddenly checking enterprise in this direction. For several years the coffee-growers fought the blight with all manner of cures and preventives, but with small success, and at length some of the less persevering abandoned coffee-growing altogether and turned their attention to more encouraging pursuits. The coffee interest has not yet recovered its former importance, but is improving slowly. The exportation of this article last year was over 268,000 pounds, and it is expected that the present year's yield will be much greater. Contrast the progress of the coffee interest with that of sugar, and the demoralizing effects of the blight upon the former will be more readily seen.

EXPORTATIONS

	1852	1865
Coffee, pounds	117,000	263,000
Sugar, pounds	730,000	15,318,097

Thus the sugar yield of last year was more than twenty times what it was in 1852, while the coffee yield has scarcely more than doubled.

The coffee plantations we encountered in our short journey looked well, and we were told that the crop was unusually promising.

There are no finer oranges in the world than those produced in the district of Kona; when new and fresh they are delicious. The principal market for them is California, but of course they lose much of their excellence by so long a voyage. About 500,000 oranges were exported last year against 15,000 in 1852. The orange culture is safe and sure, and is being more and more extensively engaged in every year. We passed one orchard that contained ten thousand orange trees.

There are many species of beautiful trees in Kona—noble forests of them—and we had numberless opportunities of contrasting the orange with them. The verdict rested with the orange. Among the varied and handsome foliage of the ko, koa, kukui, bread-fruit, mango, guava, peach, citron, ohia and other fine trees, its dark, rich green cone was sure to arrest the eye and compel constant exclamations of admiration. So dark a green is its foliage, that at a distance of a quarter of a mile the orange tree looks almost black.

The ride from Kailua to Kealakekua Bay is worth taking. It passes along high ground—say a thousand feet above sea level—and usually about a mile distant from the ocean, which is always in sight, save that occasionally you find yourself buried in the forest in the midst of rank, tropical vegetation and a dense growth of trees, whose great boughs overarch the road and shut out sun and sea and everything, and leave you in a dim, shady tunnel, haunted with invisible singing birds and fragrant with the odor of flowers. It was pleasant to ride occasionally in the warm sun, and feast the eye upon the ever-changing panorama of the forest (beyond and below us), with its many tints, its softened lights and shadows, its hillowy undulations sweeping gently down from the mountain to the sea. It was pleasant also, at intervals, to leave the sultry sun and pass into the cool, green depths of this forest and indulge in sentimental reflections under the inspiration of its brooding twilight and its whispering foliage. The jaunt through Kona will always be to me a happy memory.

MARK TWAIN

Reprinted from the Sacramento Weekly Union
August 25, 1866.

STORY OF CAPTAIN COOK

July—
1866.

AT one farmhouse we got some large peaches of excellent flavor while on our horseback ride through Kona. This fruit, as a general thing, does not do well in the Sandwich Islands. It takes a sort of almond shape, and is small and bitter. It needs frost, they say, and perhaps it does; if this be so, it will have a good opportunity to go on needing it, as it will not be likely to get it. The trees from which the fine fruit I have spoken of came had been planted and replanted over and over again, and to this treatment the proprietor of the orchard attributed his success.

We passed several sugar plantations—new ones and not very extensive. The crops were, in most cases, third rattoons. [NOTE: The first crop is called 'plant cane;' subsequent crops which spring from the original roots, without replanting are called 'rattoons.'] Almost everywhere on the island of Hawaii sugarcane matures in twelve months, both rattoons and plant, and although it ought to be taken off as soon as it tassels, no doubt, it is not absolutely necessary to do it until about four months afterward. In Kona, the average yield of an acre of ground is two tons of sugar, they say. This is only a moderate yield for these islands, but would be extraordinary for Louisiana and most other sugar-growing countries. The plantations in Kona being on pretty high ground—up among the light and frequent rains—no irrigation whatever is required.

In Central Kona there is but little idle cane land now, but there is a good deal in North and South Kona. There are thousands of acres of cane land unoccupied on the island of Hawaii, and the prices asked for it range from one dollar to a hundred and fifty an acre. It is owned by common natives, and is lying 'out of doors.' They make no use of it whatever, and yet, here lately, they seem disinclined to either lease or sell it. I was frequently told this. In this connection it may not be out of place to insert an extract from a book of Hawaiian travels recently published by a visiting minister of the gospel:

'Well, now, *I* wouldn't, if I was you.'

'Brown, I *wish* you wouldn't look over my shoulder when I am writing; and I wish you would indulge yourself in some little respite from my affairs and interest yourself in your own business sometimes.

'Well, I don't care. I'm disgusted with these mush-and-milk preacher travels, and I wouldn't make an extract from one of them. Father Damon has got stacks of books shoemakered up by them pious bushwhackers from America, and they're the flattest reading—they are sicker than the smart things children say in the newspapers. Every preacher that gets lazy comes to the Sandwich Islands to "recruit his health," and then he goes back home and writes a book. And he puts in a lot of history, and some legends, and some manners and customs, and dead loads of praise of the missionaries for civilizing and Christianizing the natives, and says in considerable chapters how grateful the savage ought to be; and when there is a chapter to be filled out, and they haven't got anything to fill it out with, they shovel in a lot of Scripture—now *don't* they? You just look at Rev. Cheever's book and Anderson's—and when they come to the volcano, or any sort of heavy scenery, and it is too much bother to describe it; they shovel in another lot of Scripture, and wind up with "Lo! what God hath wrought!" Confound their lazy melts! Now, *I* wouldn't make extracts out of no such bosh.'

'Mr. Brown, I brought you with me on this voyage merely because a newspaper correspondent should travel in some degree of state, and so command the respect of strangers; I did not expect you to assist me in my literary labors with your crude ideas. You may desist from further straining your intellect for the present, Mr. Brown, and proceed to the nearest depot and replenish the correspondent fountain of inspiration.'

'Fountain dry now, of course. Confound me if I ever chance an opinion but I've got to trot down to the soda factory and fill up that cursed jug again. It seems to me that you need more inspiration—'

'Good afternoon, Brown.'

The extract I was speaking of reads as follows:

'We were in North Kona. The arable uplands in both the Konas are owned chiefly by foreigners. Indeed, the best of the lands on all the islands appear to be fast going into foreign hands; and one of the allegations made to me by a foreign resident against the missionaries was that their influence was against such a transfer. The Rev. Mr.— told me, however, that to prevent the lands immediately about him, once owned by the admirable Kapiolani, from going to strangers he knew not who, he had felt obliged to invest his own private funds in them.'

We naturally swell with admiration when we contemplate a sacrifice like this. But while I read the generous last words of that extract, it fills me with inexpressible satisfaction to know that the Rev. Mr.— had his reward. He paid fifteen hundred dollars for one of those pieces of land; he did not have to keep it long; without sticking a spade into it he sold it to a foreigner for ten thousand dollars in gold. Yet there be those among us who fear to trust the precious promise, 'Cast thy bread upon the waters and it shall return unto thee after many days.'

I have since been told that the original $1,500 belonged to a ward of the missionary, and that inasmuch as the latter was investing it with the main view to doing his charge the best service in his power, and doubtless would not have felt at liberty to so invest it merely to protect the poor natives, his glorification in the book was not particularly gratifying to him. The other missionaries smile at the idea of their tribe 'investing their own private funds' in this free and easy, this gay and affluent way—buying fifteen hundred dollars' worth of land at a dash (salary $400 a year), and merely to do a trifling favor to some savage neighbor.

At four o'clock in the afternoon we were winding down a mountain of dreary and desolate lava to the sea, and closing our pleasant land journey. This lava is the accumulation of ages; one torrent of fire after another has rolled down here in old times, and built up the island structure higher and higher. Underneath, it is honey-combed with caves; it would be of no use to dig wells in such a place; they would not hold water—you would not find any for them to hold, for that matter. Consequently, the planters depend upon cisterns.

The last lava flow occurred here so long ago that there are none now living who witnessed it. In one place it inclosed and burned down a grove of cocoa-nut trees, and the holes in the lava where the trunks stood are still visible; their sides retain the impression of the bark; the trees fell upon the burning river, and becoming partly submerged, left in it the perfect counterfeit of every knot and branch and leaf, and even nut, for curiosity seekers of a long distant day to gaze upon and wonder at.

There were doubtless plenty of Kanaka sentinels on guard hereabouts at that time, but they did not leave casts of their figures in the lava as the Roman sentinels at Herculaneum and Pompeii did. It is a pity it is so, because such things are so interesting, but so it is. They probably went away. They went away early, perhaps. It was very bad. However, they had their merits; the Romans exhibited the higher pluck, but the Kanakas showed the sounder judgment.

As usual, Brown loaded his unhappy horse with fifteen or twenty pounds of 'specimens,' to be cursed and worried over for a time, and then discarded for new toys of a similar nature. He is like most people who visit these islands; they are always collecting specimens, with a wild enthusiasm, but they never get home with any of them.

Shortly we came in sight of that spot whose history is so familiar to every school-boy in the wide world—Kealakekua Bay—the place where Captain Cook, the great circumnavigator, was killed by the natives nearly a hundred years ago. The setting sun was flaming upon it, a Summer shower was falling, and it was spanned by two magnificent rainbows. Two gentlemen who were in advance of us rode through one of these, and for a moment their garments shone with a more than regal splendor. Why did not Captain Cook have taste enough to call his great discovery the Rainbow Islands? These charming spectacles are present to you at every turn; they are as common in all the islands as fogs and wind in San Francisco; they are visible every day, and frequently at night also—not the silvery bow we see once in an age in the States, by moonlight, but barred with all bright and beautiful colors, like the children of the sun and rain. I saw one of them a few nights ago. What the sailors call 'rain-dogs'—little patches of rainbow—are often seen drifting about the heavens in these latitudes, like stained cathedral windows.

Kealakekua Bay is a little curve like the last kink of a snail shell, winding deep into the land, seemingly not more than a mile wide from shore to shore. It is bounded on one side—where the murder was done—by a little flat plain, on which stands a cocoa-nut grove and some ruined houses; a steep wall of lava, a thousand feet high at the upper end and three or four hundred at the lower, comes down from the mountain and bounds the inner extremity of it. From this wall the place takes its name, *Kealakekua*, which in the native tongue signifies 'The Pathway of the Gods.' They say (and still believe, in spite of their liberal education in Christianity), that the great god *Lono*, who used to live upon the hillside, always traveled that causeway when urgent business connected with heavenly affairs called him down to the seashore in a hurry.

As the red sun looked across the placid ocean through the tall, clean stems of the cocoa-nut trees, like a blooming whisky bloat through the bars of a city prison, I went and stood in the edge of the water on the flat rock pressed by Captain Cook's feet when the blow was dealt that took away his life, and tried to picture in my mind the doomed man struggling in the midst of the multitude of exasperated savages—the men in the ship crowding to the vessel's side and gazing in anxious dismay toward the shore—the—But I discovered that I could not do it.

It was growing dark, the rain began to fall, we could see that the distant *Boomerang* was helplessly becalmed at sea, and so I adjourned to the cheerless little box of a warehouse and sat down to smoke and think, and wish the ship would make the land—for we had not eaten much for the ten hours and were viciously hungry.

Plain unvarnished history takes the romance out of Captain Cook's assassination, and renders a deliberate verdict of justifiable homicide. Wherever he went among the islands he was cordially received and welcomed by the inhabitants, and his ships lavishly supplied with all manner of food. He returned these kindnesses with insult and ill-treatment.

When he landed at Kealakekua Bay, a multitude of natives, variously estimated at from ten to fifteen thousand, flocked about him and conducted him to the principal temple with more than royal honors—with honors suited to their chiefest god, for such they took him to be. They called him Lono—a deity who had resided at that place in a former age, but who had gone away and had ever since been anxiously expected back by the people. When Cook approached the awe-stricken people, they prostrated themselves and hid their faces. His coming was announced in a loud voice by heralds, and those who had not time to get out of the way after prostrating themselves, were trampled under foot by the following throngs. Arrived at the temple, he was taken into the most sacred part and placed before the principal idol, immediately under an altar of wood on which a putrid log was deposited. 'This was held toward him while the priest repeated a long and rapidly enunciated address, after which he was led to the top of a partially decayed scaffolding. Ten men, bearing a large hog and bundles of red cloth, then entered the temple and prostrated themselves before him. The cloth was taken from them by the priest, who encircled Cook with it in numerous folds, and afterward offered the hog to him in sacrifice. Two priests, alternately and in unison, chanted praises in honor of Lono, after which they led him to the chief idol, which, following their example, he kissed.' He was anointed by the high priest—that is to say, his arms, hands and face, were slimed over with the chewed meat of a cocoa-nut; after this nasty compliment, he was regaled with awa manufactured in the mouths of attendants and spit out into a drinking vessel; 'as the last most delicate attention, he was fed with swine-meat which had been masticated for him by a filthy old man.'

These distinguished civilities were never offered by the islanders to mere human beings. Cook was mistaken for their absent god; he accepted the situation and helped the natives to deceive themselves. His conduct might have been wrong, in a moral point of view, but his policy was good in conniving at the deception, and proved itself so; the belief that he was a god saved him a good while from being killed—protected him thoroughly and completely, until, in an unlucky moment, it was discovered that he was only a man. His death followed instantly. Jarves, from whose history, principally, I am condensing this narrative, thinks his destruction was a direct consequence of his dishonest personation of the god, but unhappily for the argument, the historian proves, over and over again, that the false Lono was spared time and again when simple Captain Cook of the Royal Navy would have been destroyed with small ceremony.

The idolatrous worship of Captain Cook, as above described, was repeated at every heathen temple he visited. Wherever he went the terrified common people, not being accustomed to seeing gods marching around of their own free will and accord and without human assistance, fled at his approach or fell down and worshiped him. A priest attended him and regulated the religious ceremonies which constantly took place in his honor; offerings, chants and addresses met him at every point. 'For a brief period he moved among them an earthly god—observed, feared and worshiped.' During all this time the whole island was heavily taxed to supply the wants of the ships or contribute to the gratification of their officers and crews, and, as was customary in such cases, no return expected. 'The natives rendered much assistance in fitting the ships and preparing them for their voyages.'

At one time the King of the island laid a tabu upon his people, confining them to their houses for several days. This interrupted the daily supply of vegetables to the ships; several natives tried to violate the tabu, under threats made by Cook's sailors, but were prevented by a chief, who, for thus enforcing the laws of his country, had a musket fired over his head from one of the ships. This is related in Cook's *Voyages*. The tabu was soon removed, and the Englishmen were favored with the boundless hospitality of the natives as before, except that the Kanaka women were interdicted from visiting the ships; formerly, with extravagant hospitality, the people had sent their wives and daughters on board themselves. The officers and sailors went freely about the island, and were everywhere laden with presents. The King visited Cook in royal state, and gave him a large number of exceedingly costly and valuable presents—in return for which the resurrected Lono presented His Majesty a white linen shirt and a dagger—an instance of illiberality in every way discreditable to a god.

'On the 2d of February, at the desire of his commander, Captain King proposed to the priests to purchase for fuel the railing which surrounded the top of the temple of *Lono!* In this Cook manifested as little respect for the religion in the mythology of which he figured so conspicuously, as scruples in violating the divine precepts of his own. Indeed, throughout his voyages a spirit regardless of the rights and feelings of others, when his own were interested, is manifested, especially in his last cruise, which is a blot upon his memory.'

Cook desecrated the holy places of the temple by storing supplies for his ships in them, and by using the level grounds within the inclosure as a general workshop for repairing his sails, etc.—ground which was so sacred that no common native dared to set his foot upon it. Ledyard, a Yankee sailor, who was with Cook, and whose journal is considered the most just and reliable account of this eventful period of the voyage says two iron hatchets were offered for the temple railing, and when the sacrilegious proposition was refused by the priests with horror and indignation, it was torn down by order of Captain Cook and taken to the boats by the sailors, and the images which surmounted it removed and destroyed in the presence of the priests and chiefs.

The abused and insulted natives finally grew desperate under the indignities that were constantly being heaped upon them by men whose wants they had unselfishly relieved at the expense of their own impoverishment, and angered by some fresh baseness, they stoned a party of sailors and drove them to their boats. From this time onward Cook and the natives were alternately friendly and hostile until Sunday, the 14th, whose setting sun saw the circumnavigator a corpse.

Ledyard's account and that of the natives vary in no important particulars. A Kanaka, in revenge for a blow he had received at the hands of a sailor (the natives say he was flogged), stole a boat from one of the ships and broke it up to get the nails out of it. Cook determined to seize the King and remove him to his ship and keep him a prisoner until the boat was restored. By deception and smoothly-worded persuasion he got the aged monarch to the shore, but when they were about to enter the boat a multitude of natives flocked to the place, and one raised a cry that their King was going to be taken away and killed. Great excitement ensued, and Cook's situation became perilous in the extreme. He had only a handful of marines and sailors with him, and the crowd of natives grew constantly larger and more clamorous every moment. Cook opened hostilities himself.

Hearing a native make threats, he had him pointed out, and fired on him with a blank cartridge. The man, finding himself unhurt, repeated his threats, and Cook fired again and wounded him mortally. A speedy retreat of the English party to the boats was now absolutely necessary; as soon as it was begun Cook was hit with a stone, and discovering who threw it, he shot the man dead. The officer in the boats observing the retreat, ordered the boats to fire; this occasioned Cook's guard to face about and fire also, and then the attack became general. Cook and Lieutenant Phillips were together a few paces in the rear of the guard, and perceiving a general fire without orders, quitted the King and ran to the shore to stop it; but not being able to make themselves heard, and being close pressed upon by the chiefs, they joined the guard, who fired as they retreated. Cook having at length reached the margin of the water, between the fire and the boats, waved with his hat for them to cease firing and come in; and while he was doing this a chief stabbed him from behind with an iron dagger (procured in traffic with the sailors), just under the shoulder-blade, and it passed quite through his body. Cook fell with his face in the water and immediately expired.

The native account says that after Cook had shot two men, he struck a stalwart chief with the flat of his sword, for some reason or other; the chief seized and pinioned Cook's arms in his powerful gripe, and bent him backward over his knee (not meaning to hurt him, for it was not deemed possible to hurt the god *Lono*, but to keep him from doing further mischief) and this treatment giving him pain, he betrayed his mortal nature with a groan! It was his death-warrant. The fraud which had served him so well was discovered at last. The natives shouted, 'He groans!— he is not a god!' and instantly they fell upon him and killed him.

His flesh was stripped from the bones and burned (except nine pounds of it which were sent on board the ships). The heart was hung up in a native hut, where it was found and eaten by three children, who mistook it for the heart of a dog. One of these children grew to be a very old man, and died here in Honolulu a few years ago. A portion of Cook's bones were recovered and consigned to the deep by the officers of the ships.

Small blame should attach to the natives for the killing of Cook. They treated him well. In return, he abused them. He and his men inflicted bodily injury upon many of them at different times, and killed at least three of them before they offered any proportionate retaliation.

MARK TWAIN

Reprinted from the Sacramento Weekly Union
August 25, 1866.

FORAGING FOR FOOD

July —
1866

WHEN I DIGRESSED from my personal narrative to write about Cook's death I left myself, solitary, hungry and dreary, smoking in the little warehouse at Kealakekua Bay. Brown was out somewhere gathering up a fresh lot of specimens, having already discarded those he dug out of the old lava flow during the afternoon. I soon went to look for him. He had returned to the great slab of lava upon which Cook stood when he was murdered, and was absorbed in maturing a plan for blasting it out and removing it to his home as a specimen. Deeply pained at the bare thought of such sacrilege, I reprimanded him severely and at once removed him from the scene of temptation. We took a walk then, the rain having moderated considerably. We clambered over the surrounding lava field, through masses of weeds, and stood for a moment upon the door-step of an ancient ruin—the house once occupied by the aged King of Hawaii—and I reminded Brown that that very stone step was the one across which Captain Cook drew the reluctant old King when he turned his footsteps for the last time toward his ship.

I checked a movement on Mr. Brown's part: 'No,' I said, 'let it remain; seek specimens of a less hallowed nature than this historical stone.'

We also strolled along the beach toward the precipice of Kealakekua, and gazed curiously at the semi-circular holes high up in its face—graves, they are, of ancient kings and chiefs—and wondered how the natives ever managed to climb from the sea up the sheer wall and make those holes and deposit their packages of patrician bones in them.

Tramping about in the rear of the warehouse, we suddenly came upon another object of interest. It was a cocoa-nut stump, four or five feet high, and about a foot in diameter at the butt. It had lava bowlders piled around its base to hold it up and keep it in its place, and it was entirely sheathed over, from top to bottom, with rough, discolored sheets of copper, such as ships' bottoms are coppered with. Each sheet had a rude inscription scratched upon it—with a nail, apparently—and in every case the execution was wretched. It was almost dark by this time, and the inscriptions would have been difficult to read even at noonday, but with patience and industry I finally got them all in my note-book. They read as follows:

Near this spot fell
CAPTAIN JAMES COOK,
The Distinguished Circumnavigator, who Discovered
these Islands A. D. 1778.
His Majesty's Ship Imogene, *October* 17, 1837.

Parties from H. M. S. Vixen *visited this spot Jan.* 25, 1858.
This sheet and capping put on by Sparrowhawk, September 16, 1839, *in order to preserve this monument to the memory of Cook.*

Captain Montressor and officers of H.M.S. Calypso *visited this spot the* 13*th of October*, 1858.
This tree having fallen, was replaced on this spot by H.M. S.V. Cormorant, *G. T. Gordon, Esq., Captain, who visited this bay May* 18, 1846.
This bay was visited, July 4, 1843, *by* H.M.S. Carysfort, *the Right Honorable Lord George Paulet, Captain, to whom, as the representative of Her Britannic Majesty Queen Victoria, these islands were ceded, February* 25, 1843.

After Cook's murder, his second in command, on board the ship, opened fire upon the swarms of natives on the beach, and one of his cannon balls cut this cocoa-nut tree short off and left this monumental stump standing. It looked sad and lonely enough out there in the rainy twilight. But there is no other monument to Captain Cook. True, up on the mountain side we had passed by a large inclosure like an ample hog-pen, built of lava blocks, which marks the spot where Cook's flesh was stripped from his bones and burned; but this is not properly a monument, since it was erected by the natives themselves, and less to do honor to the circumnavigator than for the sake of convenience in roasting him. A thing like a guide-board was elevated above this pen on a tall pole, and formerly there was an inscription upon it describing the memorable occurrence that had there taken place; but the sun and the wind have long ago so defaced it as to render it illegible.

The sky grew overcast, and the night settled down gloomily. Brown and I went and sat on the little wooden pier, saying nothing, for we were tired and hungry and did not feel like talking. There was no wind; the drizzling, melancholy rain was still falling, and not a sound disturbed the brooding silence save the distant roar of the surf and the gentle washing of the wavelets against the rocks at our feet. We were very lonely. No sign of the vessel. She was still becalmed at sea, no doubt. After an hour of sentimental meditation, I bethought me of working upon the feelings of my comrade. The surroundings were in every way favorable to the experiment. I concluded to sing—partly because music so readily touches the tender emotions of the heart, and partly because the singing of pathetic ballads and such things is an art in which I have been said to excel. In a voice tremulous with feeling, I began:

> *'Mid pleasures and palaces though we may roam,*
> *Be it ever so humble there's no place like home;*
> *H-o-m-e—ho-home—sweet, swee-he-he—*

My poor friend rose up slowly and came and stood before me and said:

'Now look a-here, Mark—it ain't no time, and it ain't no place, for you to be going on in that way. I'm hungry, and I'm tired, and wet; and I ain't going to be put upon and aggravated when I'm so miserable. If you was to start in on any more yowling like that, I'd shove you overboard—I would, by geeminy.'

'Poor vulgar creature,' I said to myself, 'he knows no better. I have not the heart to blame him. How hard a lot is his, and how much he is to be pitied, in that his soul is dead to the heavenly charm of music. I cannot sing for this man; I cannot sing for him while he has that dangerous calm in his voice, at any rate.'

We spent another hour in silence and in profound depression of spirits; it was so gloomy and so still, and so lonesome, with nothing human anywhere near save those bundles of dry kingly bones hidden in the face of the cliff. Finally Brown said it was hard to have to sit still and starve with plenty of delicious food and drink just beyond our reach—rich young cocoa-nuts! I said, 'what an idiot you are not to have thought of it before. Get up and stir yourself; in five minutes we shall have a feast and be jolly and contented again!'

The thought was cheering in the last degree, and in a few moments we were in the grove of cocoa-palms, and their ragged plumes were dimly visible through the wet haze, high above our heads. I embraced one of the smooth, slender trunks, with the thought of climbing it, but it looked very far to the top, and of course there were no knots or branches to assist the climber, and so I sighed and walked sorrowfully away.

'Thunder! what was that!'

It was only Brown. He had discharged a prodigious lava-block at the top of a tree, and it fell back to the earth with a crash that tore up the dead silence of the palace like an avalanche. As soon as I understood the nature of the case I recognized the excellence of the idea. I said as much to Brown, and told him to fire another volley. I cannot throw lava-blocks with any precision, never having been used to them, and therefore I apportioned our labor with that fact in view, and signified to Brown that he would only have to knock the cocoa-nuts down—I would pick them up myself.

Brown let drive with another bowlder. It went singing through the air and just grazed a cluster of nuts hanging fifty feet above ground.

'Well done!' said I; 'try it again.'

He did so. The result was precisely the same.

'Well done again!' said I; 'move your hind-sight a shade to the left, and let her have it once more.'

Brown sent another bowlder hurling through the dingy air—too much elevation—it just passed over the cocoa-nut tuft.

'Steady, lad,' said I; 'you scatter too much. Now—one, two, fire!' and the next missile clove through the tuft and a couple of long, slender leaves came floating down to the earth. 'Good!' I said; 'depress your piece a line.'

Brown paused and panted like an exhausted dog; then he wiped some perspiration from his face—a quart of it, he said—and discarded his coat, vest and cravat. The next shot fell short. He said, 'I'm letting down; them large bowlders are monstrous responsible rocks to send up there, but they're rough on the arms.'

He then sent a dozen smaller stones in quick succession after the fruit, and some of them struck in the right place, but the result was—nothing. I said he might stop and rest awhile.

'Oh, never mind,' he said, 'I don't care to take any advantage—I don't want to rest until you do. But it's singular to me how you always happen to divide up the work about the same way. I'm to knock 'em down, and you're to pick 'em up. I'm of the opinion that you're going to wear yourself down to just nothing but skin and bones on this trip, if you ain't more careful. Oh, don't mind about me resting—I can't be tired—I ain't hove only about eleven ton of rocks up into that liberty pole.'

'Mr. Brown, I am surprised at you. This is mutiny.'

'Oh, well, I don't care what it is—mutiny, sass or what you please—I'm so hungry that I don't care for nothing.'

It was on my lips to correct his loathsome grammar, but I considered the dire extremity he was in, and withheld the deserved reproof.

After some time spent in mutely longing for the coveted fruit, I suggested to Brown that if he would climb the tree I would hold his hat. His hunger was so great that he finally concluded to try it. His exercise had made him ravenous. But the experiment was not a success. With infinite labor and a great deal of awkwardly-constructed swearing, he managed to get up some thirty feet, but then he came to an uncommonly smooth place and began to slide back slowly but surely. He clasped the tree with arms and legs, and tried to save himself, but he had got too much sternway, and the thing was impossible; he dragged for a few feet and then shot down like an arrow.

'It is *tabu*,' he said, sadly. 'Let's go back to the pier. The transom to my trowsers has all fetched away, and the legs of them are riddled to rags and ribbons. I wish I was drunk, or dead, or something—anything so as to be out of this misery.'

I glanced over my shoulders, as we walked along, and observed that some of the clouds had parted and left a dim lighted doorway through to the skies beyond; in this place, as in an ebony frame, our majestic palm stood up and reared its graceful crest aloft; the slender stem was a clean, black line; the feathers of the plume—some erect, some projecting horizontally, some drooping a little and others hanging languidly down toward the earth—were all sharply cut against the smooth gray background.

'A beautiful, beautiful tree is the cocoa-palm!' I said, fervently.

'I don't see it,' said Brown, resentfully. 'People that haven't clumb one are always driveling about how pretty it is. And when they make pictures of these hot countries they always shove one of the ragged things into the foreground. I don't see what there is about it that's handsome; it looks like a feather-duster struck by lightning.'

Perceiving that Brown's mutilated pantaloons were disturbing his gentle spirit, I said no more.

Toward midnight a native boy came down from the uplands to see if the *Boomerang* had got in yet, and we chartered him for subsistence service. For the sum of twelve and a half cents in coin he agreed to furnish cocoa-nuts enough for a dozen men at five minutes' notice. He disappeared in the murky atmosphere, and in a few seconds we saw a little black object, like a rat, running up our tall tree and pretty distinctly defined against the light place in the sky; it was our Kanaka, and he performed his contract without tearing his clothes—but then he had none on, except those he was born in. He brought five large nuts and tore the tough green husks off with his strong teeth, and thus prepared the fruit for use. We perceived then that it was about as well that we failed in our endeavors, as we never could have gnawed the husks off. I would have kept Brown trying, though, as long as he had any teeth. We punched the eye-holes out and drank the sweet (and at the same time pungent) milk of two of the nuts, and our hunger and thirst were satisfied. The boy broke them open and we ate some of the mushy, white paste inside for pastime, but we had no real need of it.

After a while a fine breeze sprang up and the schooner soon worked into the bay and cast anchor. The boat came ashore for us, and in a little while the clouds and the rain were gone. The moon was beaming tranquilly down on land and sea, and we two were stretched upon the deck sleeping the refreshing sleep and dreaming the happy dreams that are only vouchsafed to the weary and the innocent.

MARK TWAIN

Reprinted from the Sacramento Weekly Union
September 1, 1866.

HISTORY AND LEGEND

July — 1866.

IN MY LAST I spoke of the old cocoa-nut stump, all covered with copper plates bearing inscriptions commemorating the visits of various British naval commanders to Captain Cook's death-place at Kealakekua Bay. The most magniloquent of these is that left by 'the Right Hon. Lord George Paulet, to whom, as the representative of Her Britannic Majesty Queen Victoria, the Sandwich Islands were ceded, February 25, 1843.'

Lord George, if he is alive yet, would like to tear off that plate and destroy it, no doubt. He was fearfully snubbed by his Government, shortly afterward, for his acts as Her Majesty's representative upon the occasion to which he refers with such manifest satisfaction.

A pestilent fellow by the name of Charlton had been Great Britain's Consul at Honolulu for many years. He seems to have employed his time in sweating, fuming and growling about everything and everybody; in acquiring property by devious and inscrutable ways; in blackguarding the Hawaiian Government and the missionaries; in scheming for the transfer of the islands to the British crown; in getting the King drunk and laboring diligently to keep him so; in working to secure a foothold for the Catholic religion when its priests had been repeatedly forbidden by the King to settle in the country; in promptly raising thunder every time an opportunity offered, and in making himself prominently disagreeable and a shining nuisance at all times.

You will thus perceive that Charlton had a good deal of business on his hands. There was 'a heap of trouble on the old man's mind.'

He was sued in the courts upon one occasion for a debt of long standing, amounting to £3,000, and judgment rendered against him. This made him lively. He swore like the army in Flanders. But it was of no avail. The case was afterwards carefully examined twice—once by a Commission of distinguished English gentlemen and once by the law officers of the British Crown—and the Hawaiian Court's decision sustained in both instances. His property was attached, and one Skinner, a relative who had $10,000 in bank, got ready to purchase it when it should be sold on execution. So far, so good.

Several other English residents had been worsted in lawsuits. They and Charlton became loud in their denunciation of what they termed a want of justice in the Hawaiian Courts. The suits were all afterwards examined by the law officers of the British Crown, and the Hawaiian Courts sustained, as in Charlton's case.

Charlton got disgusted, wrote a 'sassy' letter to the King, and left suddenly for England, conferring his Consulate, for the time being, upon a kindred spirit named Simpson, a bitter traducer of the Hawaiian Government—an officer whom the Government at once refused to recognize. Charlton left with Simpson a demand upon the Government for possession of a large and exceedingly valuable tract of land in Honolulu, alleged to have been transferred to him by a deed duly signed by a native gentleman, who had never owned the property, and whose character for probity was such that no one would believe he ever would have been guilty of such a proceeding. Charity compels us to presume that the versatile Charlton forged the deed. The boundaries, if specified, were vaguely defined; it contained no mention of a consideration for value received; it had been held in abeyance and unmentioned for twenty years, and its signer and witnesses were long since dead. It was a shaky instrument altogether.

On his way to England Charlton met my Lord George in a Queen's ship, and laid his grievances before him, and then went on. My Lord sailed straight to Honolulu and began to make trouble. Under threats of bombarding the town, he compelled the King to make the questionable deed good to the person having charge of Charlton's property interests; demanded the reception of the new Consul; demanded that all those suits—a great number—which had been decided adversely to Englishmen (including many which had even been settled by amicable arbitration between the parties) should be tried over again, and by juries composed entirely of Englishmen, although the written law provided that but half the panel should be English, and therefore, of course, the demand could not be complied with without a tyrannical assumption of power by the King; he stopped the seizure and sale of Charlton's property; he brought in a little bill (gotten up by the newly-created and promptly-emasculated Consul, Simpson) for $117,000 and some odd change—enough to 'bust' the Hawaiian exchequer two or three times over—to use a popular missionary term—for all manner of imaginary damages sustained by British subjects at divers and sundry times, and among the items was one demanding $3,000 to indemnify Skinner for having kept his $10,000 lying idle for four months, expecting to invest it in Charlton's property, and then not getting a chance to do it on account of Lord George having stopped the sale. An exceedingly nice party was Lord George, take him all around.

For days and nights together the unhappy Kamehameha III was in bitterest distress. He could not pay the bill, and the law gave him no power to comply with the other demands. He and his Ministers of State pleaded for mercy—for time to remodel the laws to suit the emergency. But Lord George refused steadfastly to accede to either request, and finally, in tribulation and sorrow, the King told him to take the islands and do with them as he would; he knew of no other way—his Government was too weak to maintain its rights against Great Britain.

And so Lord George took them and set up his Government, and hauled down the royal Hawaiian ensign and hoisted the English colors over the archipelago. And the sad King notified his people of the event in a proclamation which is touching in its simple eloquence:

> *Where are you, chiefs, people and commons from my ancestors, and people from foreign lands!*
>
> *Hear ye! I make known to you that I am in perplexity by reason of difficulties into which I have been brought without cause; therefore I have given away the life of our land, hear ye! But my rule over you, my people, and your privileges will continue, for I have hope that the life of the land will be restored when my conduct is justified.*
>
> KAMEHAMEHA III

And then, I suppose, my Lord George Paulet, temporary King of the Sandwich Islands, went complacently skirmishing around his dominions in his ship, and feeding fat on glory—for we find him, four months later, visiting Kealakekua Bay and nailing *his* rusty sheet of copper to the memorial stump set up to glorify the great Cook—and imagining, no doubt, that his visit had conferred immortality upon a name which had only possessed celebrity before.

But my lord's happiness was not to last long. His superior officer, Rear-Admiral Thomas, arrived at Honolulu a week or two afterward, and as soon as he understood the case he immediately showed the new Government the door and restored Kamehameha to all his ancient powers and privileges. It was the 31st of July, 1843. There was immense rejoicing on Oahu that day. The Hawaiian flag was flung to the breeze. The King and as many of his people as could get into the Great Stone Church went there to pray, and the balance got drunk. The 31st of July is Independence Day in the Sandwich Islands, and consequently in these times there are two grand holidays in the Islands in the month of July. The Americans celebrate the 4th with great pomp and circumstance, and the natives outdo them if they can, on the 31st—and the speeches disgorged upon both occasions are regularly inflicted in cold blood upon the people by the newspapers, that have a dreary fashion of coming out just a level week after one has forgotten any given circumstance they talk about.

When I woke up on the schooner's deck in the morning, the sun was shining down right fervently, everybody was astir, and Brown was gone—gone in a canoe to Captain Cook's side of the bay, the Captain said. I took a boat and landed on the opposite shore, at the port of entry. There was a house there—I mean a foreigner's house—and near it were some native grass huts. The Collector of this port of entry not only enjoys the dignity of office, but has emoluments also. That makes it very nice, of course. He gets five dollars for boarding every foreign ship that stops there, and two dollars more for filling out certain blanks attesting such visit. As many as three foreign ships stop there in a single year, sometimes. Yet, notwithstanding this wild rush of business, the late Collector of the port committed suicide several months ago. The foreign ships which visit this place are whalers in quest of water and potatoes. The present Collector lives back somewhere—has a den up the mountain several thousand feet—but he comes down fast enough when a ship heaves in sight.

I found two Washoe men at the house. But I was not surprised; I believe if a man were to go to perdition itself he would find Washoe men there, though not so thick, maybe, in the other place.

Two hundred yards from the house were the ruins of the pagan temple of Lono, so desecrated by Captain Cook when he was pretending to be that deity. Its low, rude walls look about as they did when he saw them, no doubt. In a cocoa-nut grove near at hand is a tree with a hole through its trunk, said to have been made by a cannon-ball fired from one of the ships at a crowd of natives immediately after Cook's murder. It is a very good hole.

The high chief cook of this temple—the priest who presided over it and roasted the human sacrifices—was uncle to Obookia, and at one time that youth was an apprentice-priest under him. Obookia was a young native of fine mind, who, together with three other native boys, was taken to New England by the captain of a whaleship during the reign of Kamehameha I, and were the means of attracting the attention of the religious world to their country and putting it into their heads to send missionaries there. And this Obookia was the very same sensitive savage who sat down on the church steps and wept because his people did not have the Bible. That incident has been very elaborately painted in many a charming Sunday School book—aye, and told so plaintively and so tenderly that I have cried over it in Sunday School myself, on general principles, although at a time when I did not know much and could not understand why the people of the Sandwich Islands need care a cent about it as long as they did not know there was a Bible at all. This was the same Obookia—this was the very same old Obookia—so I reflected, and gazed upon the ruined temple with a new and absorbing interest. Here that gentle spirit worshiped; here he sought the better life, after his rude fashion; on this stone, perchance, he sat down with his sacred lasso, to wait for a chance to rope in some neighbor for the holy sacrifice; on this altar, possibly, he broiled his venerable grandfather, and presented the rare offering before the high priest, who may have said, 'Well done, good and faithful servant.' It filled me with emotion.

Obookia was converted and educated, and was to have returned to his native land with the first missionaries, had he lived. The other native youths made the voyage, and two of them did good service, but the third, Wm. Kanui, fell from grace afterward, for a time, and when the gold excitement broke out in California he journeyed thither and went to mining, although he was fifty years old. He succeeded pretty well, but the failure of Page, Bacon & Co. relieved him of $6,000, and then, to all intents and purposes, he was a bankrupt community. Thus, after all his toils, all his privations, all his faithful endeavors to gather together a competence, the blighting hand of poverty was laid upon him in his old age and he had to go back to preaching again. One cannot but feel sad to contemplate such afflictions as these cast upon a creature so innocent and deserving.

And finally he died—died in Honolulu in 1864. The Rev.

Mr. Damon's paper, referring—in the obituary notice—to Page-Bacon's unpaid certificates of deposit in the unhappy man's possession, observes that 'he departed this life leaving the most substantial and gratifying evidence that he was prepared to die.' And so he was, poor fellow, so he was. He was cleaned out, as you may say, and he was prepared to go. He was all ready and prepared—Page-Bacon had attended to that for him. All he had to do was to shed his mortal coil. Then he was all right. Poor, poor old fellow. One's heart bleeds for him.

For some time after his bereavement in the matter of finances, he helped Rev. Mr. Rowell to carry on the Bethel Church in San Francisco and gave excellent satisfaction for a man who was so out of practice. Sleep in peace, poor tired soul!—you were out of luck many a time in your long, checkered life, but you are safe now where care and sorrow and trouble can never assail you any more.

Quite a broad tract of land near that port of entry, extending from the sea to the mountain top, was sacred to the god Lono in olden times—so sacred that if a common native set his sacrilegious foot upon it it was time for him to make his will, because his time was come. He might go around it by water, but he could not cross it. It was well sprinkled with pagan temples and stocked with awkward, homely idols carved out of logs of wood. There was a temple devoted to prayers for rain—and with rare sagacity it was placed at a point so well up on the mountain side that if you prayed there twenty-four times a day for rain you would be likely to get it every time. You would seldom get to your Amen before you would have to hoist your umbrella.

And there was a large temple near at hand which was built in a single night, in the midst of storm and thunder and rain, by the ghastly hands of dead men! Tradition says that by the weird glare of the lightning a noiseless multitude of phantoms were seen at their strange labor far up the mountain side at dead of night—flitting hither and thither and bearing great lava-blocks clasped in their nerveless fingers—appearing and disappearing as the fitful lightning fell upon their pallid forms and faded away again. Even to this day, it is said, the natives hold this dread structure in awe and reverence, and will not pass by it in the night.

At noon I observed a bevy of nude native young ladies bathing in the sea, and went down to look at them. But with a prudery which seems to be characteristic of that sex everywhere, they all plunged in with a lying scream, and when they rose to the surface they only just poked their heads out and showed no disposition to proceed any further in the same direction. I was naturally irritated by such conduct, and therefore I piled their clothes up on a bowlder in the edge of the sea and sat down on them and kept the wenches in the water until they were pretty well used up. I had them in the door, as the missionaries say. I was comfortable, and I just let them beg. I thought I could freeze them out, may be, but it was impracticable. I finally gave it up and went away, hoping that the rebuke I had given them would not be lost upon them. I went and undressed and went in myself. And then they went out. I never saw such singular perversity. Shortly a party of children of both sexes came floundering around me, and then I quit and left the Pacific ocean in their possession.

I got uneasy about Brown finally, and as there were no canoes at hand, I got a horse whereon to ride three or four miles around to the other side of the bay and hunt him up. As I neared the end of the trip, and was riding down the 'pathway of the gods' toward the sea in the sweltering sun, I saw Brown toiling up the hill in the distance, with a heavy burden on his shoulder, and knew that canoes were scarce with him, too. I dismounted and sat down in the shade of a crag, and after a while—after numerous pauses to rest by the way—Brown arrived at last, fagged out, and puffing like a steamboat, and gently eased his ponderous burden to the ground—the cocoa-nut stump all sheathed with copper memorials to the illustrious Captain Cook.

'Heavens and earth!' I said, 'what are you going to do with that?'

'Going to do with it!—lemme blow a little—lemme blow—it's monstrous heavy, that log is; I'm most tired out—going to do with it! Why, I'm going to take her home for a specimen.'

'You egregious ass! March straight back again and put it where you got it. Why, Brown, I am surprised at you—and hurt. I am grieved to think that a man who has lived so long in the atmosphere of refinement which surrounds me can be guilty of such vandalism as this. Reflect, Brown, and say if it be right—if it be manly—if it be generous—to lay desecrating hands upon this touching tribute of a great nation to her gallant dead? Why, Brown, the circumnavigator Cook labored all his life in the service of his country; with a fervid soul and a fearless spirit, he braved the dangers of the unknown seas and planted the banner of England far and wide over their beautiful island world. His works have shed a glory upon his native land which still lives in her history to-day; he laid down his faithful life in her service at last, and, unforgetful of her son, she yet reveres his name and praises his deeds—and in token of her love, and in reward for the things he did for her, she has reared this monument to his memory—this symbol of a nation's gratitude—which you would defile with unsanctified hands. Restore it, go!'

'All right, if you say so; but I don't see no use of such a spread as you're making. I don't see nothing so very high-toned about this old rotten chunk. It's about the orneryest thing for a monument I've ever struck yet. If it suits Cook, though, all right;

I wish him joy; but if I was planted under it I'd highst it, if it was the last act of my life. Monument! it ain't fit for a dog—I can buy dead loads of just such for six bits. She puts this over Cook—but she put one over that foreigner—what was his name?—Prince Albert—that cost a million dollars—and what did *he* do? Why, he never done anything—never done anything but lead a gallus, comfortable life, at home and out of danger, and raise a large family for Government to board at £300,000 a year apiece. But with this fellow, you know, it was different. However, if you say the old stump's got to go down again, down she goes. As I said before, if it's your wishes, I've got nothing to say. Nothing only this—I've fetched her a mile or a mile and a half, and she weighs a hundred and fifty I should judge, and if it would suit Cook just as well to have her planted up here instead of down there, it would be considerable of a favor to me.'

I made him shoulder the monument and carry it back, nevertheless. His criticisms on the monument and its patron struck me, though, in spite of myself. The creature has got no sense, but his vaporings sound strangely plausible sometimes.

In due time we arrived at the port of entry once more.

MARK TWAIN

Reprinted from the Sacramento Weekly Union
September 8, 1866.

VOYAGE BY CANOE

July—
1866.

I HAVE BEEN WRITING a good deal, of late, about the great god Lono and Captain Cook's personation of him. Now, while I am here in Lono's home, upon ground which his terrible feet have trodden in remote ages—unless these natives lie, and they would hardly do that, I suppose—I might as well tell who he was.

The idol the natives worshiped for him was a slender, unornamented staff twelve feet long. Unpoetical history says he was a favorite god on the island of Hawaii—a great king who had been deified for meritorious services—just our own fashion of rewarding heroes, with the difference that we would have made him a Postmaster instead of a god, no doubt. In an angry moment he slew his wife, a goddess named Kaikilani Alii. Remorse of conscience drove him mad, and tradition presents us the singular spectacle of a god traveling 'on the shoulder;' for in his gnawing grief he wandered about from place to place boxing and wrestling with all whom he met. Of course this pastime soon lost its novelty, inasmuch as it must necessarily have been the case that when so powerful a deity sent a frail human opponent 'to grass' he never came back any more. Therefore, he instituted games called makahiki, and ordered that they should be held in his honor, and then sailed for foreign lands on a three-cornered raft, stating that he would return some day, and that was the last of Lono. He was never seen any more; his raft got swamped, perhaps. But the people always expected his return, and they were easily led to accept Captain Cook as the restored god.

But there is another tradition which is rather more poetical than this bald historical one. Lono lived in considerable style up here on the hillside. His wife was very beautiful, and he was devoted to her. One day he overheard a stranger proposing an elopement to her, and without waiting to hear her reply he took the stranger's life and then upbraided Kaikilani so harshly that her sensitive nature was wounded to the quick. She went away in tears, and Lono began to repent of his hasty conduct almost before she was out of sight. He sat him down under a cocoanut tree to await her return, intending to receive her with such tokens of affection and contrition as should restore her confidence and drive all sorrow from her heart. But hour after hour winged its tardy flight and yet she did not come. The sun went down and left him desolate. His all-wise instincts may have warned him that the separation was final, but he hoped on, nevertheless, and when the darkness was heavy he built a beacon fire at his door to guide the wanderer home again, if by any chance she had lost her way. But the night waxed and waned and brought another day, but not the goddess. Lono hurried forth and sought her far and wide, but found no trace of her. At night he set his beacon fire again and kept lone watch, but still she came not; and a new day found him a despairing, broken-hearted god. His misery could no longer brook suspense and solitude, and he set out to look for her. He told his sympathizing people he was going to search through all the island world for the lost light of his household, and he would never come back any more till he had found her. The natives always implicitly believed that he was still pursuing his patient quest and that he would find his peerless spouse again some day, and come back; and so, for ages they waited and watched in trusting simplicity for his return. They gazed out wistfully over the sea at any strange appearance on its waters, thinking it might be their loved and lost protector. But Lono was to them as the rainbow-tinted future seen in happy visions of youth—for he never came.

Some of the old natives believed Cook was Lono to the day of their death; but many did not, for they could not understand how he could die if he was a god.

Only a mile or so from Kealakekua Bay is a spot of historic interest—the place where the last battle was fought for idolatry. Of course we visited it, and came away as wise as most people do who go and gaze upon such mementoes of the past when in an unreflective mood.

While the first missionaries were on their way around the Horn, the idolatrous customs which had obtained in the islands as far back as tradition reached were suddenly broken up. Old Kamehameha I was dead, and his son, Liholiho, the new King, was a free liver, a roistering, dissolute fellow, and hated the restraints of the ancient *tabu*. His assistant in the Government, Kaahumanu, the Queen dowager, was proud and high-spirited, and hated the *tabu* because it restricted the privileges of her sex and degraded all women very nearly to the level of brutes. So the case stood. Liholiho had half a mind to put his foot down, Kaahumanu had a whole mind to badger him into doing it, and whisky did the rest. It was probably the first time whisky ever prominently figured as an aid to civilization. Liholiho came up to Kailua as drunk as a piper, and attended a great feast; the determined Queen spurred his drunken courage up to a reckless pitch, and then, while all the multitude stared in blank dismay, he moved deliberately forward and sat down with the women! They saw him eat from the same vessel with them, and were appalled! Terrible moments drifted slowly by, and still the King ate, still he lived, still the lightnings of the insulted gods were withheld! Then conviction came like a revelation—the superstitions of a hundred generations passed from before the people like a cloud, and a shout went up, 'The *tabu* is broken! the *tabu* is broken!'

Thus did King Liholiho and his dreadful whisky preach the first sermon and prepare the way for the new gospel that was speeding southward over the waves of the Atlantic.

The *tabu* broken and destruction failing to follow the awful sacrilege, the people, with that childlike precipitancy which has always characterized them, jumped to the conclusion that their gods were a weak and wretched swindle, just as they formerly jumped to the conclusion that Captain Cook was no god, merely because he groaned, and promptly killed him without stopping to inquire whether a god might not groan as well as a man if it suited his pleasure to do it; and satisfied that the idols were powerless to protect themselves they went to work at once and pulled them down—hacked them to pieces—applied the torch—annihilated them!

The pagan priests were furious. And well they might be; they had held the fattest offices in the land, and now they were beggared; they had been great—they had stood above the chiefs—and now they were vagabonds. They raised a revolt; they scared a number of people into joining their standard, and Kekuokalani, an ambitious offshoot of royalty, was easily persuaded to become their leader.

In the first skirmish the idolaters triumphed over the royal army sent against them, and full of confidence they resolved to march upon Kailua. The King sent an envoy to try and conciliate them, and came very near being an envoy short by the operation; the savages not only refused to listen to him, but wanted to kill him. So the King sent his men forth under Major-General Kalaimoku and the two hosts met at Kuamoo. The battle was long and fierce—men and women fighting side by side, as was the custom—and when the day was done the rebels were flying in every direction in hopeless panic, and idolatry and the *tabu* were dead in the land!

The royalists marched gayly home to Kailua glorifying the new dispensation. 'There is no power in the gods,' said they; 'they are a vanity and a lie. The army with idols was weak; the army without idols was strong and victorious!'

The nation was without a religion.

The missionary ship arrived in safety shortly afterward, timed by providential exactness to meet the emergency, and the gospel was planted as in a virgin soil.

At noon, we hired a Kanaka to take us down to the ancient ruins at Honaunau in his canoe—price two dollars—reasonable enough, for a sea voyage of eight miles, counting both ways.

The native canoe is an irresponsible looking contrivance. I cannot think of anything to liken it to but a boy's sled runner hollowed out, and that does not quite convey the correct idea. It is about fifteen feet long, high and pointed at both ends, is a foot and a half or two feet deep, and so narrow that if you wedged a fat man into it you might not get him out again. It seems to sit right upon top of the water like a duck, but it has an outrigger and does not upset easily if you keep still. This outrigger is formed of two long bent sticks, like plow handles, which project from one side, and to their outer ends is bound a curved beam composed of an extremely light wood, which skims along the surface of the water and thus saves you from an upset on that side, while the outrigger's weight is not so easily lifted as to make an upset on the other side a thing to be greatly feared. Still, until one gets used to sitting perched upon this knife-blade, he is apt to reason within himself that it would be more comfortable if there were just an outrigger or so on the other side also.

I had the bow seat, and Brown sat amidships and faced the Kanaka, who occupied the stern of the craft and did the paddling. With the first stroke the trim shell of a thing shot out from the shore like an arrow. There was not much to see. While we were on the shallow water of the reef, it was pastime to look down into the limpid depths at the large bunches of branching coral—the unique shrubbery of the sea. We lost that, though, when we got out into the dead blue water of the deep. But we had the picture of the surf, then, dashing angrily against the crag-bound shore and sending a foaming spray high into the air. There was interest in this beetling border, too, for it was honey-combed with quaint caves and arches and tunnels, and had a rude semblance of the dilapidated architecture of ruined keeps and castles rising out of the restless sea. When this novelty ceased to be a novelty, we had to turn our eyes shoreward and gaze at the long mountain with its rich green forests stretching up into the curtaining clouds, and at the specks of houses in the rearward distance and the diminished schooner riding sleepily at anchor. And when these grew tiresome we dashed boldly into the midst of a school of huge, beastly porpoises engaged at their eternal game of arching over a wave and disappearing, and then doing it over again and keeping it up—always circling over, in that way, like so many well-submerged wheels. But the porpoises wheeled themselves away, and then we were thrown upon our own resources. It did not take many minutes to discover that the sun was blazing like a bonfire, and that the weather was of a melting temperature. It had a drowsing effect, too, and when Brown attempted to open a conversation, I let him close it again for lack of encouragement. I expected he would begin on the Kanaka, and he did:

'Fine day, John.'

'Aole iki.'

[I took that to mean 'I don't know,' and as equivalent to 'I don't understand you.']

'Sorter sultry, though.'

'Aole iki.'

'You're right—at least I'll let it go at that, anyway. It makes you sweat considerable, don't it?'

'Aole iki.'

'Right again, likely. You better take a bath when you get down here to Honaunau—you don't smell good, any how, and you can't sweat that way long without smelling worse.'

'Aole iki.'

'Oh, this ain't any use. This Injun don't seem to know anything but "Owry ikky," and the interest of that begins to let down after it's been said sixteen or seventeen times. I reckon I'll bail out a while for a change.'

I expected he would upset the canoe, and he did. It was well enough to take the chances, though, because the sea had flung the blossom of a wave into the boat every now and then, until, as Brown said in a happy spirit of exaggeration, there was abont as much water inside as there was outside. There was no peril about the upset, but there was a very great deal of discomfort. The author of the mischief thought there was compensation for it, however, in that there was a marked improvement in the Kanaka's smell afterwards.

At the end of an hour we had made the four miles, and landed on a level point of land, upon which was a wide extent of old ruins, with many a tall cocoa-nut tree growing among them. Here was the ancient City of Refuge—a vast inclosure, whose stone walls were twenty feet thick at the base, and fifteen or twenty feet high; an oblong square, a thousand and forty feet one way, and a fraction under seven hundred the other. Within this inclosure, in early times, have been three rude temples; each was 210 feet long by 100 wide, and 13 high.

In those days, if a man killed another anywhere on the island the relatives of the deceased were privileged to take the murderer's life; and then a chase for life and liberty began—the outlawed criminal flying through pathless forests and over mountain and plain, with his hopes fixed upon the protecting walls of the City of Refuge, and the avenger of blood following hotly after him! Sometimes the race was kept up to the very gates of the temple, and the panting pair sped through long files of excited natives, who watched the contest with flashing eye and dilated nostril, encouraging the hunted refugee with sharp, inspirited ejaculations, and sending up a ringing shout of exultation when the saving gates closed upon him and the cheated pursuer sank exhausted at the threshold. But sometimes the flying criminal fell under the hand of the avenger at the very door, when one more brave stride, one more brief second of time would have brought his feet upon the sacred ground and barred him against all harm. Where did these isolated pagans get this idea of a City of Refuge—this ancient Jewish custom?

This old sanctuary was sacred to all—even to rebels in arms and invading armies. Once within its walls, and confession made to the priest and absolution obtained, the wretch with a price upon his head could go forth without fear or without danger—he was *tabu*, and to harm him was death. The routed rebels in the lost battle for idolatry fled to this place to claim sanctuary, and many were thus saved.

Close to a corner of the great inclosure is a round structure of stone, some six or eight feet high, with a level top about ten or twelve feet in diameter. This was the place of execution. A high palisade of cocoa-nut piles shut out its cruel scenes from the vulgar multitude. Here criminals were killed, the flesh stripped from the bones and burned, and the bones secreted in holes in the body of the structure. If the man had been guilty of a high crime, the entire corpse was burned.

The walls of the temple are a study. The same food for speculation that is offered the visitor to the Pyramids of Egypt he will find here—the mystery of how they were constructed by a people unacquainted with science and mechanics. The natives have no invention of their own for hoisting heavy weights, they had no beasts of burden, and they have never even shown any knowledge of the properties of the lever. Yet some of the lava-blocks quarried out, brought over rough, broken ground, and built into this wall, six or seven feet from the ground, are of prodigious size and would weigh tons. How did they transport and how raise them?

Both the inner and outer surfaces of the walls present a smooth front and are very creditable specimens of masonry. The blocks are of all manner of shapes and sizes, but yet are fitted together with the neatest exactness. The gradual narrowing of the wall from the base upward is accurately preserved. No cement was used, but the edifice is firm and compact and is capable of resisting storm and decay for centuries. Who built this temple, and how it was built, and when, are mysteries that may never be unraveled.

Outside of these ancient walls lies a sort of coffin-shaped stone eleven feet four inches long and three feet square at the small end (it would weigh a few thousand pounds), which the high chief who held sway over this district many centuries ago brought hither on his shoulder one day to use as a lounge! This circumstance is established by the most reliable traditions. He used to lie down on it, in his indolent way, and keep an eye on his subjects at work for him and see that there was no 'soldiering' done. And no doubt there was not any done to speak of, because he was a man of that sort of build that incites to attention to business on the part of an employee. He was fourteen or fifteen feet high. When he stretched himself at full length on his lounge, his legs hung down over the end, and when he snored he woke the dead. These facts are all attested by irrefragible tradition.

Brown said: 'I don't say anything against this Injun's inches, but I copper his judgment. He didn't know his own size. Because if he did, why didn't he fetch a rock that was long enough, while he was at it?'

On the other side of the temple is a monstrous seven-ton rock, eleven feet long, seven feet wide and three feet thick. It is raised a foot or a foot and a half above the ground, and rests upon half a dozen little stony pedestals. The same old fourteen-footer brought it down from the mountain, merely for fun (he had his own notions about fun, and they were marked by a quaint originality, as well), and propped it up as we find it now and as others may find it at a century hence, for it would take a score of horses to budge it from its position. They say that fifty or sixty years ago the proud Queen Kaahumanu used to fly to this rock for safety, whenever she had been making trouble with her fierce husband, and hide under it until his wrath was appeased. But these Kanakas will lie, and this statement is one of their ablest efforts—for Kaahumanu was six feet high—she was bulky—she was built like an ox—and she could no more have squeezed herself under that rock than she could have passed between the cylinders of a sugar mill. What could she gain by it, even if she succeeded? To be chased and abused by her savage husband could not be otherwise than humiliating to her high spirit, yet it could never make her feel so flat as an hour's repose under that rock would.

We walked a mile over a raised macadamized road of uniform width; a road paved with flat stones and exhibiting in its every detail a considerable degree of engineering skill. Some say that wise old pagan Kamehameha I planned and built it, but others say it was built so long before his time that the knowledge of who constructed it has passed out of the traditions. In either case, however, as the handiwork of an untaught and degraded race it is a thing of pleasing interest. The stones are worn and smooth, and pushed apart in places, so that the road has the exact appearance of those ancient paved highways leading out of Rome which one sees in pictures.

The object of our tramp was to visit a great natural curiosity at the base of the foothills—a congealed cascade of lava. Some old forgotten volcanic eruption sent its broad river of fire down the mountain side here, and it poured down in a great torrent from an overhanging bluff some fifty feet high to the ground below. The flaming torrent cooled in the winds from the sea, and remains there to-day, all seamed, and frothed and rippled—a petrified Niagara. It is very picturesque, and withal so natural that one might almost imagine it still flowed. A smaller stream trickled over the cliff and built up an isolated pyramid about thirty feet high, which has the resemblance of a mass of large gnarled and knotted vines and roots and stems intricately twisted and woven together.

We passed in behind the cascade and the pyramid, and found the bluff pierced by several cavernous tunnels, whose crooked courses we followed about fifty feet, but with no notable result, save that we made a discovery that may be of high interest to men of science. We discovered that the darkness in there was singularly like the darkness observable in other particularly dark places—exactly like it, I thought. I am borne out in this opinion by my comrade, who said he did not believe there was any difference, but if there was, he judged it was in favor of this darkness here.

Two of these winding tunnels stand as proof of Nature's mining abilities. Their floors are level, they are seven feet wide, and their roofs are gently arched. Their height is not uniform, however. We passed through one a hundred feet long, which leads through a spur of the hill and opens out well up in the sheer wall of a precipice whose foot rests in the waves of the sea. It is a commodious tunnel, except that there are occasionally places in it where one must stoop to pass under. The roof is lava, of course, and is thickly studded with little lava-pointed icicles an inch long, which hardened as they dripped. They project as closely together as the iron teeth of a corn-sheller, and if one will stand up straight and walk any distance there, he can get his hair combed free of charge.

Brown tried to hurry me away from this vicinity by saying that if the expected land breeze sprang up while we were absent, the *Boomerang* would be obliged to put to sea without waiting for us; but I did not care; I knew she would land our saddles and shirt-collars at Kau, and we could sail in the superior schooner *Emmeline*, Captain Crane, which would be entirely to my liking. Wherefore we proceeded to ransack the country for further notable curiosities.

MARK TWAIN

Reprinted from the Sacramento Weekly Union
September 29, 1866.

KEALAKEKUA TO KAU

June – 1866.

LEAVING THE CAVES and tunnels, we returned to the road and started in a general direction toward Honaunau, but were presently attracted by a number of holes in a bluff not more than three or four hundred yards from the place we had just left. We concluded to go up and examine them. Our native boatman, who had faithfully followed us thus far, and who must have been bearing the chief part of the heat and burden of the day, from the amount of perspiring he was doing, looked a little discouraged, I thought, and therefore we signified to him, in elaborate pantomime, that he might sit down and wait till we came back. We scrambled through a tangle of weeds which concealed great beds of black and wrinkled lava, and finally reached the low bluff. But the holes were just high enough to be out of reach. I bent a little below the lower one and ordered Brown to mount my shoulders and enter it. He said he could hold me easier than I could hold him, and I said he was afraid to go in that dark cavern alone. He used some seditious language of small consequence and then climbed up and crawled in. I suppose the fellow felt a little nervous, for he paused up there on his hands and knees and peered into the darkness for some minutes with nothing of him visible in the face of the precipice but his broad boot soles and a portion of his person which a casual acquaintance might not have recognized at a cursory glance. Then he and his boot soles slowly disappeared. I waited a minute in a state of lively curiosity; another minute with flagging curiosity as regarded the cave, but with a new born attention to the pelting sun; another long minute with no curiosity at all—I leaned drowsily against the wall. And about this time the investigator backed suddenly out of the hole and crushed me to the earth. We rolled down the slight declivity and brought up in a sitting posture face to face. I looked astonished, may be, but he looked terrified.

'It's one of them infernal old ancient graveyards!' he said.

'No? This is why the superstitious Kanaka staid behind, then?'

'Yes, likely. I suppose you didn't know that boneyard was there, else you'd have gone in yourself, instead of me. Certainly you would—Oh, of course.'

'Yes, you are right—but how is it in there, Brown? Compose yourself, lad—what did you find?'

'Oh, it's easy enough to talk, but I'm not going to prospect any more of them holes, not if I know myself, I ain't, and I think I do; it ain't right, any way, to be stirring up a dead man that's done his work and earned his rest, and besides it ain't comfortable.'

'But what did you see, Brown—what did you see?'

'I didn't see anything, at first—I only felt. It was dark as the inside of a whale in there, and I crawled about fifteen feet and then fetched up against something that was wood with my nose and skinned the end of it a little where you notice it's bloody. I felt of it with my hand, and judged it to be a canoe, and reached in and took out something and backed out till it was light enough and then I found it was a withered hand of one of them rusty old kings. And so I laid it down and come out.'

'Yes, you did "come out"—and you "come out" in something of a hurry, too. Give me a light.'

I climbed in and put the relic back into the canoe, with its fellows, and I trust the spirit of the deceased, if it was hovering near, was satisfied with this mute apology for our unintentional sacrilege.

And thus another item of patiently acquired knowledge grew shaky. We had learned, early, that the bones of great chiefs were hidden, like those of Kamehameha the Great; the information was accepted until we learned that it was etiquette to convey them to the volcano and cast them into the lakes of fire; that was relied on till we discovered that the legitimate receptacle for them was the holes in the precipice of Kealakekua; but now found that the walls of the City of Refuge contain orifices in which the bones of the great chiefs are deposited, and lo! here were more in this distant bluff!—and bones of great chiefs, too—all bones of great chiefs. The fact is, there is a lie out somewhere.

Tired and over-heated, we plodded back to the ruined temple. We were blistered on face and hands, our clothes were saturated with perspiration and we were burning with thirst. Brown ran, the last hundred yards, and without waiting to take off anything but his coat and boots jumped into the sea, bringing up in the midst of a party of native girls who were bathing. They scampered out, with a modesty which was not altogether genuine, I suspect, and ran, seizing their clothes as they went. He said they were very handsomely formed girls. I did not notice, particularly.

These creatures are bathing about half their time, I think.

If a man were to see a nude woman bathing at noonday in the States, he would be apt to think she was very little better than she ought to be, and proceed to favor her with an impudent stare. But the case is somewhat different here. The thing is so common that the white residents pass carelessly by, and pay no more attention to it than if the rollicking wenches were so many cattle. Within the confines of even so populous a place as Honolulu, and in the very center of the sultry city of Lahaina, the women bathe in the brooks at all hours of the day. They are only particular about getting undressed safely, and in this science they all follow the same fashion. They stoop down, snatch the single garment over the head, and spring in. They will do this with great confidence within thirty steps of a man. Finical highflyers wear bathing-dresses, but of course that is an affectation of modesty born of the high civilization to which the natives have attained, and is confined to a limited number.

Many of the native women are prettily formed, but they have a noticeable peculiarity as to shape—they are almost as narrow through the hips as men are.

As we expected, there was no schooner *Boomerang* at Kealakekua when we got back there, but the *Emmeline* was riding quietly at anchor in the same spot so lately occupied by our vessel, and that suited us much better. We waited until the land breeze served, and then put to sea. The land breeze begins to blow soon after the sun sets and the earth has commenced cooling; the sea breeze rushes inland in the morning as soon as the sun has begun to heat the earth again.

All day we sailed along within three to six miles of the shore. The view in that direction was very fine. We were running parallel with a long mountain that apparently had neither beginning nor end. It rose with a regular swell from the sea till its forests diminished to velvety shrubbery and were lost in the clouds. If there were any peaks we could not see them. The white mists hung their fringed banners down and hid everything above a certain well defined altitude. The mountain side, with its sharply marked patches of trees; the smooth green spaces and avenues between them; a little white habitation nestling here and there; a tapering church-spire or two thrust upward through the dense foliage; and a bright and cheerful sunlight over all—slanted up abreast of us like a vast picture, framed in between ocean and clouds. It was marked and lined and tinted like a map. So distinctly visible was every door and window in one of the white dwellings, that it was hard to believe it was two or three miles from our ship and two thousand feet above the level of the sea. Yet it was—and it was several thousand feet below the top of the mountain, also.

The night closed down dark and stormy. The sea ran tolerably high and the little vessel tossed about like a cork. About nine or ten o'clock we saw a torch glimmering on the distant shore, and presently we saw another coming toward us from the same spot; every moment or so we could see it flash from the top of a wave and then sink out of sight again. From the speed it made I knew it must be one of those fleet native canoes. I watched it with some anxiety, because I wondered what desperate extremity could drive a man out on such a night and on such a sea to play with his life—for I did not believe a canoe could live long in such rough water. I was on the forecastle. Pretty soon I began to think may be the fellow stood some chance; shortly I almost believed he would make the trip, though his light was shooting up and down dangerously, in another minute he darted across our bow and I caught the glare from his torch in my face. I sprang aft then to get out of him his dire and dreadful news.

It was a swindle. It was one of those simple natives risking his life to bring the Captain a present of half a dozen chickens.

'He has got an ax to grind.' I spoke in that uncharitable spirit of the civilized world which suspects all men's motives—which cannot conceive of an unselfish thought wrought into an unselfish deed by any man whatsoever, be he pagan or Christian.

'None at all,' said the Captain; 'he expects nothing in return—wouldn't take a cent if I offered it—wouldn't thank me for it, anyway. It's the same instinct that made them load Captain Cook's ships with provisions. They think it is all right—they don't want any return. They will bring us plenty of such presents before we get to Kau.'

I saw that the Kanaka was starting over the side again. I said:

'Call him back and give him a drink anyhow; he is wet—and dry also, maybe.'

'Pison him with that Jamaica rum down below,' said Brown.

'It can't be done—five hundred dollars' fine to give or sell liquor to a native.'

The Captain walked forward then to give some orders, and Brown took the Kanaka down stairs and 'pisoned' him. He was delighted with a species of rum which Brown had tried by mistake for claret during the day, and had afterwards made his will, under the conviction that he could not survive it.

They are a strange race, anyhow, these natives. They are amazingly unselfish and hospitable. To the wayfarer who visits them they freely offer their houses, food, beds, and often wives and daughters. If a Kanaka who has starved two days gets hold of a dollar he will spend it for poi, and then bring in his friends to help him devour it. When a Kanaka lights his pipe he only takes one or two whiffs and then passes it around from one neighbor to another until it is exhausted. The example of white selfishness does not affect their native unselfishness any more than the example of white virtue does their native licentiousness. Both traits are born in them—are in their blood and bones, and cannot be educated out.

By midnight we had got to within four miles of the place we were to stop at—Kau, but to reach it we must weather a point which was always hard to get around on account of contrary winds.

The ship was put about and we were soon standing far out to sea. I went to bed. The vessel was pitching so fearfully an hour afterward that it woke me up. Directly the Captain came down, looking greatly distressed, and said:

'Slip on your clothes quick and go up and see to your friend. It has been storming like everything for fifteen or twenty minutes, and I thought at first he was only seasick and could not throw up, but now he appears to be out of his head. He lies there on the deck and moans and says, "Poetry—poetry—oh, me." It is all he says. What the devil should he say that for? Hurry!'

Before the speech was half over I was plunging about the cabin with the rolling of the ship, and struggling frantically to get into my clothes. But the last sentence or two banished my fears and soothed me. I understood the case.

I was soon on deck in the midst of the darkness and the whistling winds, and with assistance groped my way to the sufferer. I told him I had nothing but some verses built out of alternate lines from the *Burial of Sir John Moore* and the *Destruction of the Sennacherib*, and proceeded to recite them:

THE BURIAL OF SIR JOHN MOORE

And other parties, subsequently to the Destruction of the Sennacherib

The Assyrian came down like the wolf on the fold,
The turf with our bayonets turning,
And his cohorts were gleaming in purple and gold,
And our lanterns dimly burning.

And the tents were all silent, the banners alone,
When the clock told the hour for retiring—
The lances unlifted, the trumpet unblown,
Though the foe were sullenly firing.

And the might of the Gentile, unsmote by the sword,
As his corse to the ramparts we hurried,
'Hath melted like snow in the glance of the Lord,
O'er the grave where our hero we buried.

For the Angel of Death spread his wings on the blast,
And smoothed down his lonely pillow,
And breathed in the face of the foe as he passed—
And we far away on the billow!

And the eyes of the sleepers waxed deadly and chill,
As we bitterly thought on the morrow,
And their hearts but once heaved and forever grew still,
But we spake not a word of sorrow!

And there lay the steed, with his nostril all wide,
In the grave where a Briton hath laid him,
And the widows of Ashur are loud in their wail,
And o'er his cold ashes upbraid him.

And there lay the rider, distorted and pale,
From the field of his fame fresh and gory,
With the dew on his brow and the rust on his mail—
So we left him alone in his glory!

'It is enough. God bless you!' said Brown, and threw up everything he had eaten for three days.

All day the next day we fought that treacherous point—always in sight of it but never able to get around it. At night we tacked out forty or fifty miles, and the following day at noon we made it and came in and anchored.

We went ashore in the first boat, and landed in the midst of a black, rough, lava solitude, and got horses and started to Waiohinu, six miles distant. The road was good, and our surroundings fast improved. We were soon among green groves and flowers and occasional plains of grass. There are a dozen houses at Waiohinu, and they have got sound roofs, which is well, because the place is tolerably high upon the mountain side and it rains there pretty much all the time. The name means 'sparkling water,' and refers to a beautiful mountain stream there, but they ought to divide up and let it refer to the rain also.

A sugar plantation has been started at Waiohinu, and 150 acres planted, a year ago, but the altitude ranges from 1,800 to 2,500 feet above sea level, and it is thought it will take another year for the cane to mature.

We had an abundance of mangoes, *papaias* and bananas here, but the pride of the islands, the most delicious fruit known to men, chirimoya, was not in season. It has a soft pulp, like a papaw, and is eaten with a spoon. The *papaia* looks like a small squash, and tastes like a papaw.

In this rainy spot trees and flowers flourish luxuriantly, and three of those trees—two mangoes and an orange—will live in my memory as the greenest, freshest and most beautiful I ever saw—and withal, the stateliest and most graceful. One of those mangoes stood in the middle of a large grassy yard, lord of the domain and incorruptible sentinel against the sunshine. When one passed within the compass of its broad arms and its impenetrable foliage he was safe from the pitiless glare of the sun—the protecting shade fell everywhere like a somber darkness.

In some places on the islands where the mango refused to bear fruit, a remedy suggested by the *Scientific American* has been tried with success. It consists in boring a hole in the trunk of the tree, filling the same with gunpowder and plugging it up.

Perhaps it might be worth while to try it on other fruit trees.

Speaking of trees reminds me that a species of large-bodied tree grows along the road below Waiohinu whose crotch is said to contain tanks of fresh water at all times; the natives suck it out through a hollow weed, which always grows near. As no other water exists in that wild neighborhood, within a space of some miles in circumference, it is considered to be a special invention of Providence for the behoof of the natives. I would rather accept the story than the deduction, because the latter is so manifestly but hastily conceived and erroneous. If the happiness of the natives had been the object, the tanks would have been filled with whisky.

The natives of the district of Kau have always dwelt apart from their fellow islanders—cut off from them by a desolate stretch of lava on one side and a mountain on the other—and they have ever shown a spirit and an independence not elsewhere to be found in Hawaii-nei. They are not thoroughly tamed yet, nor civilized or Christianized. Kau was the last district on the island that submitted to Kamehameha I. Two heaps of stones near the roadside mark where they killed two of the early kings of Hawaii. On both occasions these monarchs were trying to put down rebellion. They used to make their local chiefs very uncomfortable sometimes, and ten years ago, in playful mood, they made two tax collectors flee for their lives.

Most natives lie some, but these lie a good deal. They still believe in the ancient superstitions of the race, and believe in the Great Shark God and pray each other to death. When sworn by the Great Shark God they are afraid to speak anything but the truth; but when sworn on the Bible in court they proceed to soar into flights of fancy lying that make the inventions of Munchausen seem poor and trifling in comparison.

They worship idols in secret, and swindle the wayfaring stranger.

Some of the native judges and justices of the peace of the Kau district have been rare specimens of judicial sagacity. One of them considered that all the fines for adultery ($30 for each offense) properly belonged to himself. He also considered himself a part of the Government, and that if he committed that crime himself it was the same as if the Government committed it, and, of course, it was the duty of the Government to pay the fine. Consequently, whenever he had collected a good deal of money from other court revenues, he used to set to work and keep on convicting himself of adultery until he had absorbed all the money on hand in paying the fines.

The adultery law has been so amended that each party to the offense is now fined $30; and I would remark, in passing, that if the crime were invariably detected and the fines collected, the revenues of the Hawaiian Government would probably exceed those of the United States. I trust the observation will not be considered in the light of an insinuation, however.

An old native judge at Hilo once acquitted all the parties to a suit and then discovering, as he supposed, that he had no further hold on them and thus was out of pocket, he condemned the witnesses to pay the costs!

A Kau judge, whose two years' commission had expired, redated it himself and went on doing business as complacently as ever. He said it didn't make any difference—he could write as good a hand as the King could.

Brown bought a horse from a native at Waiohinu for twelve dollars, but happening to think of the horse-jockeying propensities of the race, he removed the saddle and found that the creature needed 'half-soling,' as he expressed it. Recent hard riding had polished most the hide off his back. He bought another and the animal went dead lame before we got to the great volcano, forty miles away. I bought a reckless little mule for fifteen dollars, and I wish I had him yet. One mule is worth a dozen horses for a mountain journey in the islands.

The first eighteen miles of the road lay mostly down by the sea, and was pretty well sprinkled with native houses. The animals stopped at all of them—a habit they had early acquired; natives stop a few minutes at every shanty they come to, to swap gossip, and we were forced to do likewise—but we did it under protest.

Brown's horse jogged along well enough for 16 or 17 miles, but then he came down to a walk and refused to improve on it. We had to stop and intrude upon a gentleman who was not expecting us, and who I thought did not want us, either, but he entertained us handsomely, nevertheless, and has my hearty thanks for his kindness.

We looked at the ruddy glow cast upon the clouds above the volcano, only twenty miles away, now (the fires had become unusually active a few days before), for a while after supper, and then went to bed and to sleep without rocking.

We stopped a few miles further on, the next morning, to hire a guide, but happily were saved the nuisance of traveling with a savage we could not talk with. The proprietor and another gentleman intended to go to the volcano the next day, and they said they would go at once if we would stop and take lunch. We signed the contract, of course. It was the usual style. We had found none but pleasant people on the island, from the time we landed at Kailua.

To get through the last twenty miles, guides are indispensable. The whole country is given up to cattle ranching, and is crossed and recrossed by a riddle of 'bull paths' which is hopelessly beyond solution by a stranger.

Portions of that little journey bloomed with beauty. Occasionally we entered small basins walled in with low cliffs, carpeted with greenest grass, and studded with shrubs and small trees whose foliage shown with an emerald brilliancy. One species, called the *mamona*, with its bright color, its delicate locust leaf, so free from decay or blemish of any kind, and its graceful shape, chained the eye with a sort of fascination. The rich verdant hue of these fairy parks was relieved and varied by the splendid carmine tassels of the *ohia* tree. Nothing was lacking but the fairies themselves.

As we trotted up the almost imperceptible ascent and neared the volcano, the features of the country changed. We came upon a long dreary desert of black, swollen, twisted, corrugated billows of lava—blank and dismal desolation! Stony hillocks heaved up, all seamed with cracked wrinkles and broken open from center to circumference in a dozen places, as if from an explosion beneath. There had been terrible commotion here once, when these dead waves were seething fire; but now all was motionless and silent—it was a petrified sea! The narrow spaces between the upheavals were partly filled with volcanic sand, and through it we plodded laboriously. The invincible *ohia* struggled for a footing even in this desert waste, and achieved it—towering above the billows here and there, with trunks flattened like spears of grass in the crevices from which they sprang.

We came at last to torn and ragged deserts of scorched and blistered lava—to plains and patches of dull gray ashes—to the summit of the mountain, and these tokens warned us that we were nearing the palace of the dread goddess Pele, the crater of Kilauea.

MARK TWAIN

Reprinted from the Sacramento Weekly Union
October 27, 1866.

THE KILAUEA VOLCANO

June 3d, Midnight
1866.

I SUPPOSE no man ever saw Niagara for the first time without feeling disappointed. I suppose no man ever saw it the fifth time without wondering how he could ever have been so blind and stupid as to find any excuse for disappointment in the first place. I suppose that any one of nature's most celebrated wonders will always look rather insignificant to a visitor at first, but on a better acquaintance will swell and stretch out and spread abroad, until it finally grows clear beyond his grasp—becomes too stupendous for his comprehension. I know that a large house will seem to grow larger the longer one lives in it, and I also know that a woman who looks criminally homely at a first glance will often so improve upon acquaintance as to become really beautiful before the month is out.

I was disappointed when I saw the great volcano of Kilauea (Ke-low-way-ah) to-day for the first time. It is a comfort to me to know that I fully expected to be disappointed, however, and so, in one sense at least, I was not disappointed.

As we 'raised' the summit of the mountain and began to canter along the edge of the crater, I heard Brown exclaim, 'There's smoke, by George!' (poor infant—as if it were the most surprising thing in the world to see smoke issuing from a volcano), and I turned my head in the opposite direction and began to crowd my imagination down. When I thought I had got it reduced to about the proper degree, I resolutely faced about and came to a dead halt. 'Disappointed, anyhow!' I said to myself. 'Only a considerable hole in the ground—nothing to Haleakala—a wide, level, black plain in the bottom of it, and a few little sputtering jets of fire occupying a place about as large as an ordinary potato-patch, up in one corner—no smoke to amount to anything. And these "tremendous" perpendicular walls they talk about, that inclose the crater! they don't amount to a great deal, either; it is a large cellar—nothing more—and precious little fire in it, too.' So I soliloquized. But as I gazed, the 'cellar' insensibly grew. I was glad of that, albeit I expected it. I am passably good at judging of heights and distances, and I fell to measuring the diameter of the crater. After considerable deliberation I was obliged to confess that it was rather over three miles, though it was hard to believe it at first. It was growing on me, and tolerably fast. And when I came to guess at the clean, solid, perpendicular walls that fenced in the basin, I had to acknowledge that they were from 600 to 800 feet high, and in one or two places even a thousand, though at a careless glance they did not seem more than two to three hundred. The reason the walls looked so low is because the basin inclosed is so large. The place looked a little larger and a little deeper every five minutes, by the watch. And still it was unquestionably small; there was no getting around that. About this time I saw an object which helped to increase the size of the crater. It was a house perched on the extreme edge of the wall, at the far end of the basin, two miles and a half away; it looked like a marten box under the eaves of a cathedral! That wall appeared immensely higher after that than it did before.

I reflected that night was the proper time to view a volcano, and Brown, with one of those eruptions of homely wisdom which rouse the admiration of strangers, but which custom has enabled me to contemplate calmly, said five o'clock was the proper time for dinner, and therefore we spurred up the animals and trotted along the brink of the crater for about the distance it is from the Lick House, in San Francisco, to the Mission, and then found ourselves at the Volcano House.

On the way we passed close to fissures several feet wide and about as deep as the sea, no doubt, and out of some of them steam was issuing. It would be suicidal to attempt to travel about there at night. As we approached the lookout-house I have before spoken of as being perched on the wall, we saw some objects ahead which I took for the brilliant white plant called the 'silver sword,' but they proved to be 'buoys'—pyramids of stones painted white, so as to be visible at night, and set up at intervals to mark the path to the lookout-house and guard unaccustomed feet from wandering into the abundant chasms that line the way.

By the path it is half a mile from the Volcano House to the lookout-house. After a hearty supper we waited until it was thoroughly dark and then started to the crater. The first glance in that direction revealed a scene of wild beauty. There was a heavy fog over the crater and it was splendidly illuminated by the glare from the fires below. The illumination was two miles wide and a mile high, perhaps; and if you ever, on a dark night and at a distance beheld the light from thirty or forty blocks of distant buildings all on fire at once, reflected strongly against over-hanging clouds, you can form a fair idea of what this looked like.

Arrived at the little thatched lookout-house, we rested our elbows on the railing in front and looked abroad over the wide crater and down over the sheer precipice at the seething fires beneath us. The view was a startling improvement on my daylight experience. I turned to see the effect on the balance of the company and found the reddest-faced set of men I almost ever saw. In the strong light every countenance glowed like red-hot iron, every shoulder was suffused with crimson and shaded rearward into dingy, shapeless obscurity! The place below looked like the infernal regions and these men like half-cooled devils just come up on a furlough.

I turned my eyes upon the volcano again. The 'cellar' was tolerably well lighted up. For a mile and a half in front of us and half a mile on either side, the floor of the abyss was magnificently illuminated; beyond these limits the mists hung down their gauzy curtains and cast a deceptive gloom over all that made the twinkling fires in the remote corners of the crater seem countless leagues removed—made them seem like the camp-fires of a great army far away. Here was room for the imagination to work! You could imagine those lights the width of a continent away—and that hidden under the intervening darkness were hills, and winding rivers, and weary wastes of plain and desert—and even then the tremendous vista stretched on, and on, and on!—to the fires and far beyond! You could not compass it—it was the idea of eternity made tangible—and the longest end of it made visible to the naked eye!

The greater part of the vast floor of the desert under us was as black as ink, and apparently smooth and level; but over a mile square of it was ringed and streaked and striped with a thousand branching streams of liquid and gorgeously brilliant fire! It looked like a colossal railroad map of the State of Massachusetts done in chain lightning on a midnight sky. Imagine it—imagine a coal-black sky shivered into a tangled net-work of angry fire!

Here and there were gleaming holes twenty feet in diameter, broken in the dark crust, and in them the melted lava—the color a dazzling white just tinged with yellow—was boiling and surging furiously; and from these holes branched numberless bright torrents in many directions, like the 'spokes' of a lady's fan, and kept a tolerably straight course for a while and then swept round in huge rainbow curves, or made a long succession of sharp worm-fence angles, which looked precisely like the fiercest jagged lightning. These streams met other streams, and they mingled with and crossed and recrossed each other in every conceivable direction, like skate tracks on a popular skating ground. Sometimes streams twenty or thirty feet wide flowed from the holes to some distance without dividing—and through the opera glasses we could see that they ran down small, steep hills and were genuine cataracts of fire, white at their source, but soon cooling and turning to the richest red, grained with alternate lines of black and gold. Every now and then masses of the dark crust broke away and floated slowly down these streams like rafts down a river. Occasionally the molten lava flowing under the superincumbent crust broke through—split a dazzling streak, from five hundred to a thousand feet long, like a sudden flash of lightening, and then acre after acre of the cold lava parted into fragments turned up edgewise like cakes of ice when a great river breaks up, plunged downward and were swallowed in the crimson cauldron. Then the wide expanse of the 'thaw' maintained a ruddy glow for a while, but shortly cooled and became black and level again. During a 'thaw,' every dismembered cake was marked by a glittering white border which was superbly shaded inwards by aurora borealis rays, which were a flaming yellow where they joined the white border, and from thence toward their points tapered into glowing crimson, then into a rich, pale carmine, and finally into a faint blush that held its own a moment and then dimmed and turned black. Some of the streams preferred to mingle together in a tangle of fantastic circles, and then they looked something like the confusion of ropes one sees on a ship's deck when she has just taken in sail and dropped anchor—provided one can imagine those ropes on fire.

Through the glasses, the little fountains scattered about looked very beautiful. They boiled, and coughed, and spluttered, and discharged sprays of stringy red fire—of about the consistency of mush, for instance—from ten to fifteen feet into the air, along with a shower of brilliant white sparks—a quaint and unnatural mingling of gouts of blood and snow-flakes!

We had circles and serpents and streaks of lightning all twined and wreathed and tied together, without a break throughout an area more than a mile square (that amount of ground was covered, though it was not strictly 'square'), and it was with a feeling of placid exultation that we reflected that many years had elapsed since any visitor had seen such a splendid display—since any visitor had seen anything more than the now snubbed and insignificant 'North' and 'South' lakes in action. We had been reading old files of Hawaiian newspapers and the 'Record Book' at the Volcano House, and were posted.

I could see the North Lake lying out on the black floor away off in the outer edge of our panorama, and knitted to it by a webwork of lava streams. In its individual capacity it looked very little more respectable than a schoolhouse on fire. True, it was about nine hundred feet long and two or three hundred wide, but then, under the present circumstances, it necessarily appeared rather insignificant, and besides it was so distant from us. We heard a week ago that the volcano was getting on a heavier spree than it had indulged in for many years, and I am glad we arrived just at the right moment to see it under full blast.

I forgot to say that the noise made by the bubbling lava is not great, heard as we heard it from our lofty perch. It makes three distinct sounds—a rushing, a hissing, and a coughing or puffing sound; and if you stand on the brink and close your eyes it is no trick at all to imagine that you are sweeping down a river on a large low-pressure steamer, and that you hear the hissing of the steam about her boilers, the puffing from her escape-pipes and the churning rush of the water abaft her wheels. The smell of sulphur is strong, but not unpleasant to a sinner.

We left the lookout-house at ten o'clock in a half-cooked condition, because of the heat from Pele's furnaces, and wrapping up in blankets (for the night was cold) returned to the hotel. After we got out in the dark we had another fine spectacle. A colossal column of cloud towered to a great height in the air immediately above the crater, and the outer swell of every one of its vast folds was dyed with a rich crimson luster, which was subdued to a pale rose tint in the depressions between. It glowed like a muffled torch and stretched upward to a dizzy height toward the zenith. I thought it just possible that its like had not been seen since the children of Israel wandered on their long march through the desert so many centuries ago over a path illuminated by the mysterious 'pillar of fire.' And I was sure that I now had a vivid conception of what the majestic 'pillar of fire' was like, which almost amounted to a revelation.

It is only at very long intervals that I mention in a letter matters which properly pertain to the advertising columns, but in this case it seems to me that to leave out the fact that there is a neat, roomy, well furnished and well kept hotel at the volcano, would be to remain silent upon a point of the very highest importance to any one who may desire to visit the place. The surprise of finding a good hotel in such an outlandish spot startled me considerably more than the volcano did. The house is new—built three or four months ago—and the table is good. One could not easily starve here even if the meats and groceries were to give out, for large tracts of land in the vicinity are well paved with excellent strawberries. One can have as abundant a supply as he chooses to call for. There has never, heretofore, been anything in this locality for the accommodation of travelers but a crazy old native grass hut, scanty fare, hard beds of matting and a Chinese cook.

MARK TWAIN

Reprinted from the Sacramento Weekly Union
November 17, 1866.

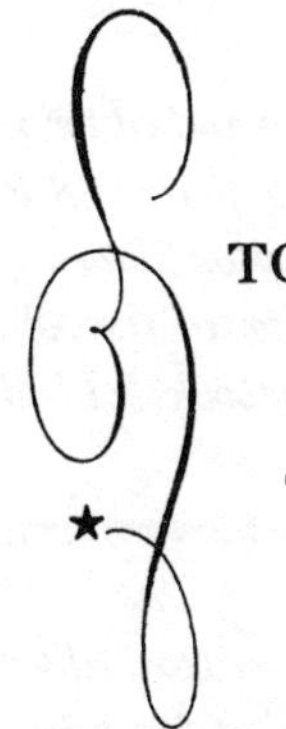

CONCLUSION TO MARK TWAIN'S LETTERS FROM THE SANDWICH ISLANDS

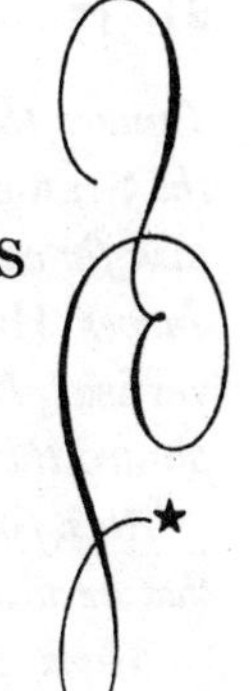

BY G. EZRA DANE

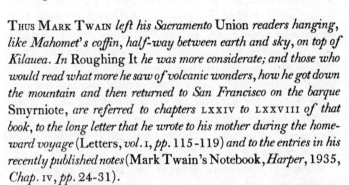

THUS MARK TWAIN *left his Sacramento* Union *readers hanging, like Mahomet's coffin, half-way between earth and sky, on top of Kilauea. In* Roughing It *he was more considerate; and those who would read what more he saw of volcanic wonders, how he got down the mountain and then returned to San Francisco on the barque* Smyrniote, *are referred to chapters* LXXIV *to* LXXVIII *of that book, to the long letter that he wrote to his mother during the homeward voyage* (Letters, *vol.* I, *pp.* 115-119) *and to the entries in his recently published notes* (Mark Twain's Notebook, *Harper*, 1935, *Chap.* IV, *pp.* 24-31).

The Honolulu press had paid no attention to Mark Twain's arrival beyond the inclusion of that strange name with the more prosaic ones on the Ajax *passenger list. His departure did not pass so unnoticed. The friendship and compliments of the distinguished Minister Burlingame had doubtless contributed to his prestige, and issues of the Sacramento* Union *containing his provocative* Letters *had begun to arrive. Reprinted in part in the Honolulu papers, they were causing quite a stir.*

The Commercial Advertiser *resented the ridicule heaped upon such officials as the unfortunate Harris and accused Mark Twain of spreading lies about the Islands and their government. "Father"*

Damon, the venerable pastor of the Seamen's Mission and editor of the Seaman's Friend, *humorously took the visiting journalist to task for carrying off a volume borrowed from the Mission library—Jarves'* History of the Sandwich Islands. *The editor of the* Advertiser, *Whitney, said that he had not only stolen the book, but had pirated the contents in his* Letters.

Alas, poor Whitney, he found out to his regret, like many others, that he was tossing pebbles at a tiger.

Mark Twain found an opportunity to devour the unwary editor in a letter to the rival Daily Hawaiian Herald. *Dated at San Francisco, Sept. 24th,* 1866, *and printed in the* Herald *of October* 17*th, his communication tells of the Hawaiian Queen Emma's arrival in San Francisco on her way back to the Islands after a tour abroad. "A crowd of gaping American kings," says Mark Twain, "beseiged the Occidental Hotel and peered anxiously into every carriage that arrived and criticized every woman that emerged from it. Not a lady arrived from the steamer but was taken for Queen Emma, and her personal appearance subjected to remarks—some of them flattering and some otherwise."*

Having disposed of the Queen in her "suite of neatly decorated apartments" at the Occidental, the correspondent took a crack in passing at John Quincy Adams Warren, who had come over from the Islands to exhibit at the Sacramento Fair "a hundred thousand varieties of lava and worms and vegetables and other valuables that he had collected in Hawaii-nei." Mark Twain professed great surprise at this gentleman's lack of gratitude for the fame he had acquired from a paragraph in one of the Sandwich Island Letters.

But the heavy ammunition was reserved for Mr. Whitney. Mark Twain led into this attack through mention of the "Great Steamer Colorado" *which the China Mail Company was making ready for service, and which would probably touch at Honolulu on her first voyage. "I expect to go out in her," said Mark, "in order to see that everything is done right . . . I am going chiefly, however, to eat the editor of the* Commercial Advertiser *for saying I do not write the truth about the Hawaiian Islands, and for exposing my highway robbery in carrying off Father Damon's book*—History of the Islands. *I shall go there mighty hungry. Mr. Whitney is jealous of me because I speak the truth so naturally, and he can't do it without taking the lock-jaw. But he ought not to be jealous; he ought not to try to ruin me because I am more virtuous than he is.* I *cannot help it—it is my nature to be reliable, just as it is his to be shaky on matters of fact—we cannot alter these natures—us leopards cannot change our spots. Therefore, why growl?—why go and try to make trouble? If he cannot tell when I am writing seriously and when I am burlesquing—if he sits down solemnly and takes one of my palpable burlesques and reads it with a funereal aspect, and swallows it as petrified truth—how am I going to help it? I cannot give him the keen perception that nature denied him—now can I? Whitney knows that. Whitney knows he has done me many a kindness, and that I do not forget it, and am still grateful—and he knows that if I could scour him up so that he could tell a broad burlesque from a plain statement of fact, I would get up in the night and walk any distance to do it. You know that, Whitney. But I am coming down there mighty hungry—most uncommonly hungry, Whitney.*"

The appetite of his voracious youth craved more than the blood of editors. This taste of foreign travel had aroused his ambition. He wanted the whole world now; nothing less than a tour around the world would satisfy his yearning imagination. The purpose shows through the facetious threats in the Herald *letter. He must go west across the Pacific to Japan and China in the new China Mail steamer, leaving in January; then on to Singapore, India, Suez, Palestine, Egypt, Europe. . . . But now he was not even secure against the bare needs of his stomach. He was out of a job again.*

From a period of distressful retirement at San Francisco he emerged with two new manuscripts and a daring plan. One manuscript, his revised account of the Hornet *disaster, was dispatched to* Harper's Magazine*—his ill-fated bid for literary distinction. The other was the text of a lecture on the Sandwich Islands. And therein lay the plan which he advanced with some trepidation—to capitalize further on his Sandwich Island trip and the publicity gained from his widely copied* Letters *by giving a public lecture on the subject. Artemus Ward had gained fame and considerable fortune in that way. His drolleries had even captivated London. Sam Clemens knew that his own ideas were at least as funny as Ward's in print, and he had felt the power of his conversation over small audiences. Why couldn't he entertain larger ones as well, and make them pay for it?*

How he was encouraged by his friend Col. John McCoomb of the Alta California *(who was later to sponsor the* Innocents Abroad *excursion); how he hired Maguire's Academy of Music for the evening of October 2d,* 1866, *and advertised, "Doors open at* 7 *o'clock; the trouble to begin at* 8;*" the fearful anticipation, the anguish of the first moments; the melting and complete surrender of the audience to alternate rolls of laughter at his burlesques of Kanaka life and silent thrills at the poetic imagery in his descriptions of Hawaiian scenery, culminating with the vast crater of Haleakala; the complete and overwhelming success and acclaim that completed the absorption of Sam Clemens' identity into that of the public character, Mark Twain—all this has been told by him in* Roughing It *(Chapters* LXXVIII *and* LXXIX*) and in a more orderly way by Mr. Paine in his great* Biography *(Chap.* LIV*). These also tell how, after the manner of new celebrities, he acquired a manager in the person of the bibulous Dennis McCarthy, who had been his employer on the* Enterprise*; and how they duplicated the San Francisco success in Sacramento, Marysville, the mining towns of Grass Val-*

ley, Nevada City, Red Dog, and (sweetest of all) in his old stronghold, Virginia City. Then at Carson, and back to San Francisco on the crest of the wave, to sign up with General McCoomb as traveling correspondent for the Alta California *on the trip around the world that was to merge into the famous Holy Land excursion.*

The point of it all here is the importance in Mark Twain's life of the Sandwich Islands tour of which you have read in this book. It launched him on the career of traveling correspondent that produced Innocents Abroad *and with it world-wide fame as an author within two years. It provided the subject and material with which he started the parallel career of lecturer that contributed at least as much as his writings to his eventual fame and popularity. For the Sandwich Island lecture was not only his first, but in one form or another it was his surest standby and chief reliance for years. He took New York with it on May 6, 1867, at Cooper Institute, just before the departure of the* Quaker City. *He carried it about the United States on various lecture tours. And he used it successfully to sustain his reputation and to capture a critical London audience when on Oct. 7, 1873, he lectured at "Hanover Square Rooms" on "Our Fellow Savages of the Sandwich Islands." His purpose was thus announced in a letter to the editor of the London* Evening Standard, *copied on the other side of the world, with some sour remarks, by his old enemy the editor of the Honolulu* Commercial Advertiser, *from whose files we have it:*

> Sir:—In view of the prevailing frenzy concerning the Sandwich Islands, and the inflamed desire of the public to acquire information concerning them, I have thought it well to tarry yet another week in England, and deliver a lecture upon this absorbing subject. And lest it be thought unbecoming in me, a stranger, to come to the public rescue at such a time, instead of leaving to abler hands a matter of so much moment, I desire to explain that I do it with the best of motives and the most honorable intentions. I do it because I am convinced that no one can allay this unwholesome excitement as effectually as I

can; and to allay it, and allay it as quickly as possible, is surely the one thing that is absolutely necessary at this juncture. I feel and know that I am equal to this task, for I can allay any kind of an excitement by lecturing upon it. I have saved many communities in this way. I have always been able to paralyze the public interest in any topic I chose to take hold of and elucidate with all my strength.

Hoping that this explanation will show that if I am seeming to intrude, I am at least doing it from a high impulse,

I am, sir, your obedient servant,

Mark Twain

He had been less modest in stating his accomplishments to the more unsophisticated citizens of Nevada City.

After the lecture is over, [he had advertised in the Nevada *Transcript*, October 23, 1866] the lecturer will perform the following wonderful feats of

SLEIGHT OF HAND

(if desired to do so)

At a given signal, he will go out with any gentleman and take a drink. If desired, he will repeat this unique and interesting feat — repeat it until the audience are satisfied that there is no more deception about it.

At a moment's warning, he will depart out of town and leave his hotel bill unsettled. He has performed this ludicrous feat many hundreds of times, in San Francisco, and elsewhere, and it has always elicited the most enthusiastic comments.

At any hour of the night after ten, the lecturer will go through any house in the city, no matter how dark it may be, and take an inventory of its contents and not miss as many of the articles as the owner will in the morning.

The lecturer declines to specify any more of his miraculous feats at present, for fear of getting the police too much interested in his circus.

And the Sacramento public had been lured to the Metropolitan Theatre by this astonishing display:

For only one night! And only a portion of that!

MARK TWAIN

Will deliver a

LECTURE

on the

SANDWICH ISLANDS

at the Metropolitan Theatre, on Thursday . . . . . October 11th.

THE CELEBRATED BEARDED WOMAN!

is not with this Circus.

The Wonderful

COW WITH SIX LEGS!

is not attached to this menagerie.

That curious and unaccountable Freak of Nature,

THE IRISH GIANT!

who stands 9 feet 6 inches in height and has a breadth of beam in proportion, and who has been the pet of kings and the honored associate of the nobility and gentry of the old world, will not be present and need not be expected.

THE KING OF THE ISLANDS!

Failed to arrive in season for the lecture in San Francisco, but may be confidently expected on this occasion.

Doors open at 7 p. m.—The Trouble to begin at 8.

In these burlesques the "Wild Humorist of the Pacific Slope" was having his last fling. Mark Twain's humor of the Enterprise, Golden Era *and* Californian *days was soon to be toned down. The* Letters from the Sandwich Islands *are of the transition period. In them he discovered beauty, but still mingled it startlingly with the broad burlesque and sometimes crude satire which theretofore had been his principal stock in trade. Doubtless a good deal of it would not have appeared in this book if he (and "Livy") had had the editing of it. Certainly he would have improved its literary quality. But for us, as it stands, it has other qualities of value. It has the vigor, fresh enthusiasm and unrestraint of the youth that Mark Twain the old man mourned. It embodies an experience that was always sweet in his memory. As all of us have done, he longed to recapture the sweetness of that experience by a return to the scenes of his youthful adventures. "If I could have my way about it," he said on one occasion, "I would go back there and remain the rest of my days. It is paradise for an indolent man. If a man is rich he can live expensively, and his grandeur will be respected as in other parts of the earth; if he is poor he can herd with the natives, and live on next to nothing; he can sun himself all day long under the palm trees, and be no more troubled by his conscience than a butterfly would.*

"When you are in that blessed retreat, you are safe from the turmoil of life; you drowse your days away in a long deep dream of peace; the past is a forgotten thing, the present is heaven, the future you leave to take care of itself. You are in the center of the Pacific Ocean; you are two thousand miles from any continent; you are millions of miles from the world; as far as you can see, on any hand, the crested billows wall the horizon; and beyond this barrier the wide universe is but a foreign land to you and barren of interest." (*N. Y.* Tribune, *Jan.* 6, 1873.)

He thus concluded a lecture on the Islands, delivered in New York in 1877: *"The land that I have tried to tell you about lies out there in the midst of the watery wilderness, in the very heart of the limitless solitudes of the Pacific. It is a dreamy, beautiful, charming land. I wish I could make you comprehend how beautiful it is. It is a land that seems ever so vague and fairy-like when one reads about it in books. It is Sunday land, the land of indolence and dreams, where the air is drowsy and lulls the spirit to repose and peace, and to forgetfulness of the labor and turmoil and weariness and anxiety of life."* (Modern Eloquence, *Thos. B. Reed, ed.*, 1900, *Vol.* IV, *pp.* 253-259.)

Perhaps it was in his mind a shrine of the dear dead happiness and lost illusions of youth, to which he was destined never to return. That westward journey around the world which he had promised himself in 1866 *did not come until twenty-nine years later, and then it was not the adventure of an eager youth, but the heavy task of honor of an old man—a world-wide lecture tour undertaken to pay off a crushing burden of debt—a last resource against the shame of bankruptcy. On that voyage Honolulu was to be the first stop, and he looked forward to the visit as a source of refreshment to his weary spirit—as though perhaps he might draw again from the coral strands some of the joyful vigor and confidence he had brought there so many years before.*

"*On the seventh day out we saw a dim vast bulk standing up out of the wastes of the Pacific and knew that that spectral promontory was Diamond Head, a piece of this world which I had not seen before for twenty-nine years. So we were nearing Honolulu, the capital city of the Sandwich Islands—those islands which to me were Paradise; a Paradise which I had been longing all those years to see again. Not any other thing in the world could have stirred me as the sight of that great rock did.*

"*In the night we anchored a mile from shore. Through my port I could see the twinkling lights of Honolulu and the dark bulk of the mountain-range that stretched away right and left. I could not make out the beautiful Nuuanu valley, but I knew where it lay, and remembered how it used to look in the old times .....*

"*Many memories of my former visit to the islands came up in my mind while we lay at anchor in front of Honolulu that night. And pictures—pictures—pictures—an enchanting procession of them! I was impatient for the morning to come.*

"*When it came it brought disappointment, of course. Cholera had broken out in the town, and we were not allowed to have any communication with the shore. Thus suddenly did my dream of twenty-nine years go to ruin.*" (Following the Equator, *Chap.* III.)

Conclusion

Probably it was better so. The old man who sailed away sadly on the Warrimoo *was wiser than the young man who had landed eagerly from the* Ajax. *His knowledge of life was vastly greater—and his estimation for it infinitely less. Is not this incident symbolic? There could be no return to youth. He had gone too far to recapture the carefree, boisterous spirit of the young man who, on June* 7, 1866, *in the Volcano House on top of Kilauea, after reading the trite sentiments expressed in the Visitors' Book, had added his own comments in characteristic burlesque, with which (as preserved in the* Daily Hawaiian Herald *for Dec.* 5, 1866) *we may appropriately take leave of him:*

Volcano House,
Thursday, June 7, 1866.

Like others who came before me I arrived here. I travelled the same way I came, most of the way. But I knew that there was a protecting Providence over us all, and I felt no fear. We have had a good deal of weather. Some of it was only so-so (and to be candid, the remainder was similar).

Mr. Brown.—But however, details of one's trifling experiences during one's journey thither may not always be in good taste in a book designed as a record of volcanic phenomena; therefore let us change to the proper subject.

Visited the crater, intending to stay all night, but the bottle containing the provisions got broke and we were obliged to return. But while we were standing near the South Lake—say 250 yards distant—we saw a lump of dirt about the size of a piece of chalk. I said in a moment, 'There is something unusual going to happen.' But soon afterwards we observed another clod of about the same size; it hesitated—shook—and then let go and fell into the lake.

Oh, God! It was awful.

We then took a drink.

Few visitors will ever achieve the happiness of two such experiences as the above in succession.

While we lay there, a puff of gas came along, and we jumped up and galloped over the rough lava in the most ridiculous manner, leaving our blankets behind. We did it because it is fashionable, and because it makes one appear to have had a thrilling adventure.

We then took another drink. After which we returned and camped a little closer to the Lake.

I mused and said, 'How the stupendous grandeur of this magnificently terrible and sublime manifestation of celestial power doth fill the poetic soul with grand thoughts and grander images; and how the overpowering solemnity' [Here the gin gave out. In the careless hands of Brown the bottle broke.]